the lazy
COUPONER

the *the* lazy COUPONER

How to Save $25,000 Per Year
in Just 45 Minutes Each Week
with No Stockpiling, No Item
Tracking, and No Sales Chasing!

Jamie Chase

RUNNING PRESS
PHILADELPHIA · LONDON

ISBN 978-0-7624-4291-1
Library of Congress Control Number: 2011925651

E-book ISBN 978-0-7624-4357-4

9 8 7 6 5 4
Digit on the right indicates the number of this printing

Cover and interior design by Amanda Richmond
Edited by Kristen Green Wiewora
Typography: Gotham and Archer

Running Press Book Publishers
2300 Chestnut Street
Philadelphia, PA 19103-4371

Visit us on the web!
www.runningpress.com

For Frank W. Jackson
and Joanie, too.

I'd like to thank:

Justin, for believing in my earliest idea, setting up the computer table, designing www.lazycouponer.com, and for so many other reasons, including Poppy Joan.

Jeff Silberman and Frank Weimann at the Literary Group for pursuing my written word and for wonderful representation. John Paine, for his word refining and willingness to gamble on me, and Elyse Tanzillo for dealing with John and me. Special thanks to Diane Mancher of One Potata Productions.

Greg Jones, Craig Herman, and Kristen Green Wiewora at Perseus, along with Nicole De Jackmo, Donna Gambale, Rick Monteith, Amanda Richmond, and Alice Sullivan for turning my manuscript into a reality.

Matt Mendolera at Matter Communications, the Extra Care Team, and CVS Pharmacies for what began as an inquiry and transitioned into a relationship.

Jay Blackman, for his post-Olympic in-flight reading, along with Natalie Morales, Paul Green, and Jeff Kleinman of the NBC gang who made the *Nightly News* segment possible. Also, the team from ABC News 6, Taryn Plumb and Mary Schwaim of the *Boston Globe*, and Lynn Hendricks and Jim Vaiknoras of the *Newburyport Daily News*, without all of whom the Literary Group would not have pursued me.

Mary Shattuck, Ernie Greenslade, and Vanessa Pepin at NECC for employment, encouragement, and promotion.

And for support in many kinds, I thank the Amesbury Public Library, all the gals at Newburyport Pediatric, Nick Ault, Drake Bennett, Larry Bucyk, Chris and Jeanette Cattan, Dick and Paula Chase, Leonidas Fernandez, Emily Fichera, Kathryn Goulet, Cindy Giusti, Tim Jackson, Cathy MacDonald of Catalina Marketing, Kunal Patel, and my awesome coupon buddy, Jenn Peetz.

Finally, I need to thank Derek and Bradley Chase for being patient; now we can play.

Table of Contents

Introduction

WELCOME TO THE WORLD OF COUPONING—a wonderful place where numbers are your friends. That's because these numbers add up in your favor until you're saving over $25,000 a year. By what means? You guessed it: couponing! Now you understand why "coupon" earns the right to be a verb. *The Lazy Couponer* will teach you how to save that kind of money in just 45 minutes a week. That's right, 45 minutes to save more than $25,000. The money I save is a rough estimate per year, post-taxes, and if I can do it, so can you.

I am terribly lazy, so once you learn my techniques, I suspect you'll do even better. After you have a solid foundation of couponing, you can choose how much of what you've learned you want to use. Go full throttle or easy breezy; it's up to you.

My methods are unique: no chasing sales, no stockpiling, and no tracking prices. Instead, *The Lazy Couponer* will teach you the simple steps to maximizing your coupons in the shortest amount of time. You'll also learn easy strategies such as "scenario-building" where you can stack coupons together and hopefully turn expenditures into profit. With scenario-building, I will show you how to combine your coupons so, like me, you can make a $167.00 grocery run and pay only $0.42 cents.

NBC NIGHTLY NEWS

When I decided to cut and use my first coupon, I had no idea that it would lead to thousands of dollars in savings, teaching college coupon classes, or being featured on the *NBC Nightly News*, but the fact that it's all happened is a testament to people's desire to save. Being a smart shopper, however, doesn't have to mean a lot of work, which is demonstrated on the *Nightly News* clip where Natalie Morales and the NBC crew documented as I clipped coupons, organized and shopped—paying $0.42 for over a week's worth of groceries. And in case you're thinking that I spent many hours prepping for the shopping trip to get my total so low, you should know the shoot was rescheduled three times and we only confirmed the film date the day before. Short time and a little organization is all that's needed to realize incredible savings, and that's why Brian Williams called me, "The Master."

While other couponers preach about running from store to store in order to catch every sale and buying massive stockpiles of items when they're marked down, I encourage you to include coupons almost effortlessly in your already hectic everyday life. I'll further show you how to skip "stockpiling shackles" and render yourself free by gifting or donating what you don't need. Furthermore, reading this book will help you achieve huge savings while avoiding mail-in rebates or, worse, the sales chase. You know what I say about chasing? "Who has all that time and energy? There will always be another sale!" That's the kind of spirit that I encourage on this couponing journey. You'll be able to turn your savings into actual cash back, making cashiers blink in amazement.

How will you incorporate an extra five-figure income into your lifestyle without going to an office? In my family, the savings enabled my husband to make a career change, leaving his successful sales job to teach at a college full-time—a job that paid considerably less but enriched our family tenfold. *The Lazy Couponer* shows you how you can make your own life richer. The students in my couponing classes range in age from 20 to 86 and come from all sorts of economic backgrounds. Each has his or her own reason for taking the class and making my methods work for them, so I am certain there is something in here for you.

Even if you only save 10% on every purchase you make, that is a tremendous bonus to your income, especially if you are continually wondering where all your money went. Or maybe you're already tracking every penny. Then I will help you turn each penny into two through the magic of couponing.

Couponing is often associated with scrimping and saving to make ends meet, but there is an ever-expanding subculture that takes pride in smart shopping regardless of means, just as one of my students learned firsthand when Natalie Morales, of *The Today Show*, flashed her own wallet stuffed with coupons! Maybe you live quite comfortably but value savings and smart economic choices. This book can show you how to make the most of your buying opportunities and use your savings to enjoy other pursuits.

The beauty of these easy methods is that they will save you time and simplify your life because you'll be saving on the items you already buy. Couponing can make you realize how inexpensively you can purchase healthy or organic foods, too.

Couponing doesn't just stop at the grocery store; I'll guide you through many other types of retail stores so that you can enjoy huge savings on household and personal items, toys, and even gifts. That's right. My Christmas spending this year for my family of four was under $100— and that included Wii games for my sons and Brooks Brothers™ clothing for my husband. How much do you think I spent one month for $400 in household and personal items? Nothing. The stores actually paid me a $60 check! Yes, you read that correctly. I made money on my purchases, products including Huggies® diapers, Gillette® razors, Nivea body wash, and more.

My savings philosophy challenges the old adage "there's no such thing as a free lunch." Not only do I get many basic necessities for free, but I also often come out ahead in the process. Factoring in my time spent on savings, I make roughly $640 an hour. If I can do it, why can't you? Maybe you thought it wasn't possible or didn't know how. Well, I am the real-world example. And *The Lazy Couponer* is your guide.

CHAPTER 1:

Couponing A to Z
(Learning the Language)

IF YOU ARE CONSIDERING COUPONING, THEN THE place to start is with our language. Using coupons is more than just cutting them from the Sunday paper and going to the store. It's about saving both money and time. And since saving time means using shortcuts, my world of couponing is full of shortcuts and abbreviations. By gaining a small mastery of our vernacular, you'll be able to make comprehensive lists, find and organize your coupons, and navigate coupon websites much easier and faster. I will also show you why it is so important to learn these abbreviations and provide real examples where using them has helped me organize and save time. The abbreviations we use are sort of a coupon-shorthand, and are worth knowing. So I'll spend most of this chapter introducing them to you. But don't get too intimidated; this is a short chapter, and the rest of the book is about saving money, coupons, and how to use them. Trust me, once you get the hang of it, this shorthand will become your best friend. You may even thank me.

So let's get started. They say a picture is worth a thousand words. Look at the picture on the next page. Can you guess my cost?

I made this purchase at CVS in February. I was trying to buy Valentine's Day cards for my son's preschool, and I did not want to pay for them. So, along with my Sunday paper, I had to figure out a scenario to make those items free. The presale price for everything you see in the photo was $113.36. So what did I pay?

I paid NOTHING! In fact, this is an example of how I *make* money shopping. My total after my purchase was $7.59 *back* in CVS **ExtraBucks**, or CVS's version of store credit. In the couponing world, we refer to purchases like this as a **money maker (MM)**. The trick is to combine coupons in such a way that you earn store credits (or actual money). Whether one penny or $20, it's money makers and **over-ages**—credits you get after your purchase price is already zero—that are key to saving when you don't have any coupons to apply.

Still not sold? Here's how I did it.

QTY	ITEM	PRESALE	SALE	COUPONS	EXTRA CARE Bucks (ECBs) earned
2	DiGiorno Pizza®	$7.78	$6.00	$8.00	
1	Huggies Wipes®	$3.49	$3.00	$2.50	
1	Sun Newspaper	$1	$1.75	$1.75	$ —
2	CVS® Paper Plates	$7.98	$ 3.99	$1.00	
2	Dove® Body Wash	$10.98	$10.98	$2.00	$10.98
1	Colgate® MaxFresh®	$3.29	$2.99	$1.75	$2.00
2	Pringles®	$4.58	$3.00	$1.00	
2	Valentine's Sets	$ 5.98	$ 2.99	$ —	
6	Coke 12 packs	$32.34	$22.00	$6.00	$10.00
7	M&M's® 12 oz	$27.93	$21.97	$4.00	$8.00
1	Stacy's® Pita Chips	$3.29	$3.29	$4.29	
	Bottle Deposits	$3.60	$3.60	$ —	
	Tax	$0.37	$0.37	$—	
	CVS Trans Qs	$—	$—	$14.00	
	Subtotals	$113.36	$85.93	$44.54	$30.98
	Sale Savings		$27.43		
	Coupons (Qs) Used			$44.54	

$31.49   Used ExtraCare Bucks (started with $18 ECBs and used an additional $13.49)

$7.59   TOTAL = MONEY MAKER (MM) with Out of Pocket (OOP) $9.90 and earned an additional $17.49 ECBs

You may not understand how this works now, but by the end of this book, you'll be making runs just like this! But first, you have to understand what all those abbreviations and funky terms actually mean. To make it quicker for you to learn, I am including a cheat sheet of terms for you at the end of this chapter (see page 23). Refer to it as you go along, and the learning process will become incredibly easy!

Just in case you are wondering what you would do with all those products, let me tell you where mine went. Remember, I don't believe in the hassle of stockpiling, so the Valentine's Day cards and the M&M's® went to my son Derek's preschool, making his classmates happy—and my husband sad. I dropped the pizzas at a neighbor's house because her husband was away on Army drill. Two pizzas were perfect for her and her young son. We used the household items, and I kept the chips for my house. Embarrassingly, I admit the soda was for me. It's my vice and I drank every last can with secret glee. Well, that is except for one case that also accompanied the pizzas to the neighbor's house. (She only got the Coke Zero® and not the yummy full-sugar stuff.)

Scenarios

Scenarios are a way to maximize savings by combining different types of coupons, sales or promotions, or cash register tapes (store credits) and by utilizing fillers: items less than $2.00 that hike up transaction totals to meet the minimum specified on the transaction coupon. Some-times, scenarios include instant rebates.

Here is a scenario where I combined four different kinds of coupons on two items: diapers and a Lindt chocolate. For now it doesn't matter what sort of coupons I used or how I combined them, because you'll learn that throughout the book; it only matters that the coupons outnumbered the items. See if you can follow it here:

Bought
   Huggies® diapers, $19.99
   Lindt, $0.25
   Subtotal: $20.24
Used
   –$5.00 Store Transaction Q
   –$3.00/1 Huggies Q
   –$1.00/1 Store diaper Q
   –$2.00/1 Store Q, on any baby product
   Buy 1 diaper, Receive $10.00 store credit back.
   Final Cost: +$0.76 Money Maker!

By expertly combining my Qs, I saved almost $20.00 on diapers alone. I didn't just get them cheaply—or free—but actually turned that diaper purchase into a money maker.

Recently, a student from one of my couponing classes asked me for some help buying Cetaphil®, a moisturizing lotion, that she needed for her daughter. The student knew the item was on sale at CVS for $10.99, but she couldn't figure how to increase her savings beyond that, because she couldn't find any coupons for it. Most couponers would never pay merely the sale price for an item, but how, she asked, do you save more? Easy. I asked her to consider purchasing additional items I knew she could really use, because that would help her bring her overall cost down. More items, less money.

Here is the breakdown of what I advised:

BUY
Cetaphil®, $10.99
Store-brand Ibuprofen, $3.99
Colgate® Toothpaste 4oz, $2.99
(3) PowerBar Pure and Simple Bars, $0.99
Subtotal: $20.94 + tax

USE/GET
-$5/$20 Trans Q
-$5.00/1 Cetaphil IP
-$1.00/1 Colgate Total Toothpaste MQ
Buy 1 CVS® Ibuprofen, Receive $3.00 ECBs (Limit 1)
Buy 1 PowerBar, Receive $0.99 ECBs (Limit 3)
Buy 1 Colgate Toothpaste, Receive $2.00 ECBs
 (Limit 2)
Final Cost: $1.97 = $9.94 OOP,
Receive $7.97 Extra Bucks

By preparing a great scenario, my techniques saved her $9.00 off her original cost and also got her five other products for free! Let's look at the first coupon line and talk it out:

$5/$20 Trans Q

$5/$20 is a **transaction coupon** (**Trans Q**) that I used to get $5.00 off the entire purchase. The minimum threshold I needed to reach to use the coupon was $20.00.
Now look at the next two coupon lines in the Cetaphil transaction:

$5.00/1 Cetaphil® IP
$1.00/1 Colgate® Total® Toothpaste MQ

To understand these **manufacturer coupons (MQs)**, you need to know that **IP** means **Internet Printable**, which is really just any coupon you print off an Internet site. The Colgate® coupon is an actual paper coupon, not an IP, so we need to cut it from a newspaper insert, such as Smart-Source.

Now let's look at all the shortcuts that involve **ExtraCare Bucks (ECBs)**:

Buy 1 CVS® Ibuprofen, Receive $3.00 ECBs (Limit 1)
Buy 1 PowerBar, Receive $0.99 ECBs (Limit 3)
Buy 1 Colgate Toothpaste, Receive $2.00 ECBs (Limit 2)

These three promotions are offered only at CVS. ECBs are CVS's version of store money awarded when you purchase trigger-items using your ExtraCare Card—or CVS loyalty card. (Yes, I'll show you how to get one on page 154.) You can use the ECBs for future transactions at CVS. You see what they're doing? They're offering the ECBs so you shop at CVS next time.

CVS sets a limit on every ExtraBuck promotion, so you can check the circulars to know how many items you can buy before you stop earning ECBs. Here, the ibuprofen earns $3.00 only one time. So you buy only one bottle. The Colgate® toothpaste earns $2.00 apiece if you buy up to two tubes. The PowerBars earn $0.99 each up to three bars. However, since we were only using the Colgate® toothpaste and PowerBars to raise the transaction total to $20.00 so she could use the $5/$20 transaction coupon, I suggested she buy only one tube of toothpaste.

The earned ECBs in her actual transaction totaled $7.97. Let's review the final line in the scenario:

Final Cost: $1.97 = $9.94 OOP,
Receive $7.97 Extra Bucks

No, **OOP** isn't a mistake. It stands for "Out of Pocket" expense. It is the actual money paid at the register. The scenario used a combination of different types of coupons—a **store coupon (SQ)** and two **manufacturer coupons (MQs)**—along with ECBs to buy the products at a cost lower than the original item, the Cetaphil®, she wanted. If you subtract the $7.97 in earned ECBs from her out-of-pocket payment of $9.94, you'll find a grand total of $1.97 for the six items. So, do you think you might want to learn more about couponing abbreviations?

COMMON COUPON TERMS

Fillers: Items that cost less than $2 (<$2 in shorthand) used to raise your transaction total to qualify for $5/$20 or other transaction coupons.

MM: Money maker—an item or transaction that yields overage, and leads to those sweet moments when you make money.

OV/OVR: Overage, earning discounts higher than the product price through combining different types of coupons.

YMMV: Your mileage may vary. Depending on where you shop, you may earn more or less for your coupons. Sale prices may also differ.

On coupon blogs or in our own personal lists, we master couponers would never write out **ExtraCare Bucks**, **Transaction Coupon**, or **Out of Pocket** expense. If you wanted to know how to replicate our scenarios, you must know the abbreviations: **ECBs, TQ,** or **OOP.** Remember, this book is about savings—money and time—so you need to learn the language, then make it your own. It doesn't take long!

The clever thing about couponing is sometimes you don't even have to use coupons to save money, but you have to understand the couponing world in order to get the savings. In essence, you must think like a couponer. I can't imagine anything lazier than couponing without coupons, can you? Nevertheless, it works, and from time to time you may find yourself at a store with none in hand as I did earlier.

Needing trash bags and cold medicine after a week with a sick household, I ran to Rite Aid®. The trash bags I usually buy are $5.49, the children's cold medicine was $5.99, and the DayQuil® I wanted was on sale for $4.00. So, I expected to pay $15.48 for the three items I set out to buy, but when I got the store I grabbed a flyer and noticed this promotion on the back cover:

With my acquired couponing skills, I quickly realized it was cheaper to get two boxes of trash bags than the one I planned, as they were on a **Buy One Get One (BOGO)** sale, and that by combining the trash bags with other items, the other items became free, like the Edy's® ice cream that was earning Rite Aid® store coupons called **UPs.** Then I broke my transaction in two, buying three Edy's®, one Gatorade®, and two trash bags in a single transaction. I paid $15.46 and earned $11.00 in UPs, $2 for each of the three Edy's, and $5 for reaching the $15 of participating product threshold outlined in the previous ad. Next, I gave the cashier my DayQuil® ($4.00), children's cold medicine ($5.99), and another Gatorade® ($1.00), and paid with the UPs I had earned moments before. So although I entered the store with no coupons in hand, preparing to pay $15.48, I actually left the store with all the items I originally wanted plus an extra box of trash bags, three gallons of ice cream, and two bottles of Gatorade® for exactly two cents less. While coupon success begins with the language, it can be so much more. Now that we've talked about couponing verbiage, the next few chapters will familiarize you with this mindset.

KNOW YOUR Q JARGON?

Here's a short quiz to help you remember the important points in this chapter. Yes, I could have written out a boring list of "Important Points to Remember," but this is way more fun. I'll put a quiz at the end of every chapter, so sharpen your pencil.

1. **What does Q mean?**
   a. Coupon!
   b. Quick
   c. Quarter

2. **What do I teach?**
   a. Preschool
   b. High school math
   c. College classes about couponing

3. **Why should you sometimes buy items you don't actually need or want?**
   a. To get those things you do want really cheap or even free.
   b. To start a massively intrusive stockpile.
   c. To annoy cashiers.

4. **What is a coupon scenario?**

    a. A coupon that can be used at Rite Aid® when purchasing the product and can also be combined with a manufacturer coupon for the product.

    b. A method of maximizing savings by combining store and manufacturer coupons, item and transaction coupons, sales or promotions, cash register tapes, and by utilizing fillers.

    c. A couponing problem.

5. **What are Q, MQ, SQ, TQ and IP abbreviations for?**

    a. Coupon, Manufacturer Coupon, Store Coupon, Transaction Coupon, and Internet Printable.

    b. Coupon, Manufacturer Coupon, Sale Coupon, Transaction Coupon, and Internet Price.

    c. Coupon, Manufacturer Coupon, Store Coupon, Transaction Coupon, and Internet Price.

Answers: 1. a, 2. c, 3. a, 4. b, 5. a

Abbreviation and Key Term Cheat Sheet

$3/1 or $.75/2: Indicates the value of a coupon—here the first is $3.00 off 1 item, the second is $0.75 cents off 2 items

$5/$20, $5 off $20—Transaction coupon (TQ): Used to get $5.00 off the entire sale when you reach the minimum transaction total of $20.00

10/$10: A sale promotion where ten items cost $10, or each item is on sale for $1.00

Ad-Perk/VV: Rite Aid® (RA) printable store coupons, also called Video Values (VV) that you earn and print after watching product videos on the Ad-perk site

B3G$2 OYNO: Refers to a promotion, where you must buy a set amount of items to get dollars off on your next order (OYNO)—here it is Buy 3 items, Get $2.00 OYNO

Blinkie: Little machine with a blinking light next to products attached to the aisle at grocery store that spits out coupons

BOGO/B1G1: Buy one get one free (B2G1—buy 2, get 1)

CAT/CATs: Also known as "Catalinas" after Catalina Marketing Company who distributes them—a CAT is a coupon printed on cash register tape or printer dispensers next to registers that helps you earn dollars off your next order (OYNO)

CRT: Cash register tape—a coupon printed at the end of a store's receipt or from a price scanner

DND: Does not double—coupons that do not qualify for double savings

Doublers: Special promotional coupons issued by stores to use with a manufacturer coupon that double the value of the manufacturer coupon

EB/ECBs: ExtraBucks or ExtraCare Bucks—the CVS® version of cash register tape store money and can be used to pay for future purchases

ES: Ever Saver – Walgreens' monthly rebate booklet

ETS: Excludes trial size

FAR: Free after rebate

FEBs: Free with ExtraBucks

Fillers: Items costing less than $2 used to get transaction totals up in order to qualify for transaction coupon minimum amounts

Freebie: A free item

FVQ: Full-value coupons, or coupons for "free items"

GBT: The CVS® green bag tag that gets scanned with the use of a reusable bag and earns $1ECB for every 4 scans

GC: Gift Card

GM: General Mills—usually the General Mills Everyday Saver newspaper insert

In-Ad: Coupon found printed within a store's flyer or circular

IP/IPs: Internet Printables—coupons printed off the Internet

Item Q: Any coupon related to a single product—can be either a store or manufacturer coupon

MB2 (MB3): Must buy two, must buy three, etc.

MFR/MANU/MAN: Manufacturer

MIR: Mail-in rebate

MM: Money Maker—an item or transaction that yields money or store credit back for you

MQ/ManuQ: A manufacturer coupon

OOP: Out of pocket expense—actual money paid out during a purchase at the register

OV/OVR: Overage—when coupons or coupon combinations are valued higher than the cost of product or products and can be applied to other items in the purchase

OYNO: On your next order/transaction

P&G/PG: Proctor & Gamble—usually the Proctor & Gamble newspaper insert

Peelies: Coupons stuck to an item that peel off

POS: Point of sale

PSA: Prices starting at

PSP: Pre-sale price

Q: A coupon!

Qdb/QDb: Coupon database

RA: Rite Aid®

RC: Coupon barcode that indicates the coupon is a Rite Aid® store coupon, not a true manufacturer coupon

Rolling Multiple transactions: using coupons earned in the one transaction to be used in the next transaction, and so on

RP: RedPlum™—usually the RedPlum newspaper insert

RR: Register Rewards Catalina program offered at Walgreens (Wags)—RRs are like Wags store money and get printed as OYNO coupons on cash register tape

S$25G10%: Indicates a promotion where you must spend a set amount to get a percent off your total, usually in the same transaction—here it is spend $25 to get 10% off

S$25G5: Indicates a promotion where you must spend a set amount to get money back, usually in OYNO Qs—here it is spend $25 to get $5 back

Scenario: A method of maximizing savings by combining man-ufacturer coupons, item and transaction coupons, sales or pro-motions, cash register tapes, and by utilizing fillers

SCR: Single Check Rebate is an online or mail-in rebate pro-gram offered at Rite Aid®

SQ: A store coupon

SS: SmartSource—usually the SmartSource newspaper insert

Stacking: The process of using any combination of store and manufacturer or different types of coupons together in order to realize the maximum savings

Tags/Taggies: Coupons that hang off an item for sale

Tearpad: Block/pad of tear-off coupons, usually at grocery stores

Trans Q/TQ: Transaction coupons are coupons used to apply a percentage or specific dollar amount off the total purchase transaction when the specified threshold is reached

TRU: Toys"R"Us

V: Valassis—usually the Valassis newspaper insert

Wags: Walgreens

Winetag: Coupon tag hanging off beer or wine bottles for dollars off meat or other companion foods

WYB: "When you buy"

YMMV: "Your mileage may vary"—accounts for regional variances in coupon value or differences in coupon acceptance or prices at different stores

CHAPTER 2:
Getting to Know Coupons

YOU KNOW WHAT A COUPON IS. BY NOW, I'M sure you've seen hundreds. You probably even know that many come in the Sunday newspaper. You might even remember as a kid watching your mother cut them from the paper to bring along while shopping. To most, a coupon is simply the $0.50 savings off a bag of chips, but to me it represents free food—produce, staples, and snacks. How? I can combine it with a CAT (Catalina marketing promotion) or BOGO (buy one get one) sale to get overage for my other products. Do you have a coupon for $1.00 off Hasbro games? Coupons like that used during a gift card sale or with a mail-in rebate can mean free gifts. Toys and video gaming—Wii, Transformers, and Leapster®—can be bought entirely with coupons. You can buy discounted clothing from retailers like Talbots®, Old Navy®, and Gymboree®, and personal care items like diapers, body wash, and razors with coupons.

Have you ever been in line watching the person in front of you use two coupons for one pack of diapers? That person knows that there is a difference between manufacturer and store coupons and also knows how to combine them. Even more amazing, the diaper shopper could have used three coupons on that single pack. She could have added a transaction coupon to take additional money off the top. Maybe you've seen a $200 grocery order brought down to merely $30 and thought, "No way. That has to take hours to achieve." Let me assure you that savings like that take only minutes a week.

Everything begins with learning what you don't now know about coupons. Why? Well, let me tell you: in order to be a smart couponer, you must first learn how to use coupons themselves, including how to properly read them, categorize them by type, and determine which stores will accept them. Next, you should learn about the retail stores where you shop so that you understand store policies and build strong working relationships with store managers and employees. These first steps may seem elementary, but they are the sticking points where most new couponers get lost.

You can't just cut out coupons from the Sunday inserts and run out the door; you really need to understand what a coupon says before you can use it. Coupon values apply differently depending on their producer, their type, bar codes, and possibly the exceptions written in fine print. Furthermore, not all stores accept coupons in the same ways, so you need to know each individual store's coupon policy as well. You can't really understand the value of a coupon unless you also consider where you are using it. This knowledge of coupons and related store use is the basis to your couponing success.

This is why it is so important to know your coupon basics well. Without strong fundamentals, you'll never see savings over 30%. (No, 30% is not enough; don't argue with me. You'll agree with me later.)

BUY ONLY WHAT YOU NEED

Inserts contain coupons for all sorts of products, so you have to exercise discipline in order to realize savings.

Marcia ran from store to store using coupons for all kinds of products her family didn't need. Before long, she had filled an entire closet with unnecessary junk. Eventually Marcia came to realize that each product in her closet represented money that she wouldn't have otherwise spent. Just because an item is on sale or you have a coupon for it doesn't mean it will translate to savings for you unless you need that product. Otherwise, you are spending money on things you wouldn't have bothered to buy in the first place.

Part I: The Coupons

Coupons are more than they first appear to be, so knowing how to read them is extremely important. I've had students in my master classes who've couponed for years but fail at this basic step. One woman couldn't understand why her overall savings for groceries, toys, clothing, and household items never broke 25%. She had been couponing for just over eighteen months and was not making any further progress. The reason: she did not know the difference between store and manufacturer coupons, and that simple but crucial mistake prevented her from doubling her savings.

First of all, when reading coupons, read the words, don't look at the picture. A picture on a coupon may show a product that's like the one you need to buy, but not be the exact product the words state. You must match the coupon words against a product. For example, look at this coupon for $1.00 off any Colgate® toothpaste. Notice that the 6.0 oz. size is pictured, but the coupon is for any size from 4.0 oz. up. You'll also notice that only three types of toothpaste are pictured (Max Fresh™, Total® Whitening, and Sensitive), but what if you prefer such Colgate® toothpastes like Colgate® 2in1, Luminous, Sparkling, Baking Soda & Peroxide, or any of the others Colgate produces which aren't pictured? The coupon says, "any Colgate Toothpaste," so the coupon would apply to all

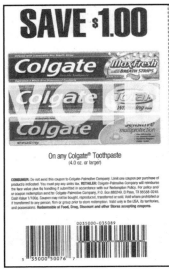

of them, even *Dora the Explorer* and other kids toothpastes. When reading coupons, look for product size, any limitations (like "limit six") or restrictions (like **DND–do not double**), expiration date, and coupon type.

Imagine you spend each Sunday cutting out those little coupons. You will feel defeated, and likely quit the couponing game all together, if you mistakenly grab the wrong product and the cashier denies you the use of the coupon. Or, you get to the register and then realize you are at the wrong store and the coupon you have with you doesn't apply. The experience is more than frustrating; often, it is humiliating. While most cashiers are encouraging about coupons, others are indifferent, and still others are rude. At some point, you will inevitably encounter a grouchy cashier who thinks (1) you are an inherent thief, (2) you must be lying or cheating the system, and (3) you have all the free time in the world to spend clipping coupons, and thus the cashier resents you for it. As a smart consumer, you should prepare yourself through knowledge about coupons and smart couponing techniques. A friendly person who knows what she is talking about will end up better off than someone surprised by what she didn't bother to read.

What are the differences you should look for? There are only two categories of coupons: store and manufacturer coupons. One is a coupon that is limited only to one retail chain; the other can be used wherever you're shopping (as long as they accept manufacturer coupons). Let's begin with the most common type of coupons: the ones offered by the manufacturers.

Manufacturer Coupons (MQ)

Manufacturer coupons are usually distributed by the parent companies of smaller brands, such as ConAgra Foods for Peter Pan®. Manufacturer coupons pertain to specific items, like candy bars or ravioli. By offering money off, the manufacturer hopes that you will choose to buy its product over its competitor's product. For example, a manufacturer coupon that reads $0.50 off a one-pound bag of New England® Coffee is distributed by New England Coffee, enticing you, as the consumer, to purchase that brand over a competitor's brand, like Dunkin Donuts® coffee.

I am a Dunks girl myself, though from time to time, I have been known to drink either New England Coffee's Columbian Supremo or Wolfgang Puck's delicious Breakfast in Bed blend. And if I were to find a New England Coffee coupon like the one pictured on the last page, I might just switch my coffee selection and pick up some of that Colombian Supremo. Then the manufacturer coupon succeeds by getting me to purchase their product. The point is: manufacturer coupons relate to a *manufacturer's* item(s).

> ## SALE COMING
> Once a manufacturer coupon is marketed to the general public, you can expect to see the related item or a direct competitor's similar item on sale any time within the next four weeks. If you don't need it immediately, hold on and wait for the sale.

Generally, manufacturer coupons are the ones you find in newspaper inserts—those little booklets in Sunday papers squished between the comic strips and the sale ads for cars and real estate. It's the entire collection of inserts and sale flyers that falls to your feet when you lift the newspaper to the checkout counter.

The manufacturer does this kind of marketing in hopes of encouraging you to purchase a specific brand. Proctor and Gamble companies are so skilled in marketing their manufacturer coupons that Proctor and Gamble actually sends out its own monthly insert just for its products. General Mills also produces a mass marketing insert, but with less regularity. Once a coupon is used against a product, the coupon is submitted from the store back to the manufacturer for reimbursement, and, through coded barcodes, the manufacturer can measure how many people used them to judge how its marketing campaign worked.

Right now you may only be familiar with the coupons

you find in the Sunday newspaper inserts, but coupons are everywhere. Just walk through your grocery store and look around for manufacturer coupons. Along with product placement, you'll start to notice giant pads of coupons called **Tearpads** that are placed right beside the product, sticking out of the shelf. Tearpads look like small notebooks and you can pull off one or two coupons as you shop. There are apple-sized square coupon machines called **Blinkies** that spit out little square **Qs** (coupons) as you pull the coupons from the machine. They're known as Blinkies because of the blinking light on top of the machine. You may even notice **Tags** or **Taggies**, which are the coupons hanging off bottles or jars. Manufacturer coupons can also come in the mail from a direct mailing promotion, on checkout receipts **(CRTs)** during point-of-purchase, or downloaded from a variety of Internet sources, including the manufacturer's own website.

BRAND LOYALTY

Bradley's eyes opened when he finally realized the differences between store and manufacturer coupons. He was so excited by how many manufacturer coupons were available to him that now he receives emails from the websites of all his favorite brands. While Bradley only buys the brands he wants and doesn't chase irrelevant sales, with his coupons in hand, he still saves tons of money!

Manufacturer coupons also benefit the stores where you shop. Once a store returns a manufacturer coupon for reimbursement, the manufacturer returns not only the coupon amount but also an extra 8¢ to the store. It's always crazy to me when a cashier huffs under her breath in irritation at my coupon use. "Really?" I want to say. "Don't you realize your

> store actually makes MORE money off my purchase because I used a coupon?"

Store Coupons (SQs)

A store coupon is one that individual stores, not manufacturers, send out to consumers. The intention of a store coupon is to provide an incentive for buyers to shop at one store rather than at its competitor. For example, much like a Vlasic® coupon ensures that you'll buy Vlasic® pickles over Claussen® pickles, Whole Foods® issues product coupons so you'll shop there instead of at Trader Joe's®. While no manufacturer reimburses the retailer for its store coupon, they gain by drawing you into their store, where you will likely purchase other items that are not on sale.

Store coupons can either be a particular amount off a specific item to purchase at the store, such as the $0.75 off Thai Kitchen® Product at Whole Foods® pictured on the opposite page, or a percentage off a single item, such as the pictured Gap® coupon.

A store coupon may also entitle you to a dollar amount off the total, like the Old Navy® coupon, or a percentage off the total, such as this pictured Lowes® 10% coupon.

Store coupons can also be for a free item, as is often the case with restaurant coupons. In my Sunday paper this past week, there was a set of coupons for both Burger King® and Friendly's®. Since they are both store coupons, they can therefore be redeemed only at their respective restaurants. For Friendly's, a family-friendly restaurant chain known best for its ice cream, the coupon offered a free kid's meal with purchase of an adult entrée. The Burger King coupon was also for a free item, the Original Chicken Sandwich, with the purchase of an Original Chicken Sandwich Value Meal. You'll notice that with both the Burger King® and the Friendly's coupons, we are really discussing examples of Buy One Get One coupons. You must first buy an item to get another item for free, so we call them BOGO store coupons. Some are more explicitly presented as BOGO coupons, like the Walgreens coupon seen here.

Store coupons are issued by all types of retailers, from major chain stores to your local mom & pop stores. The international natural and organic grocer Whole Foods Market, the specialty children's clothing chain Gymboree®, and the national discount retailer Target®® are various examples of retailers that produce internal coupons to be used only at their stores. Also, all three major national pharmacy chains—CVS®, Rite Aid®, and Walgreens®—offer store coupons to their consumers. Traditional retailers, like clothing stores, department stores, and supercenters, also produce and market store coupons through various marketing methods including newspaper inserts, Internet sites, in-store promotion books, and in-flyer ads. You simply have to look.

MQ versus SQ: Differentiating Between the Two

At first, it may seem difficult to tell whether a coupon is a manufacturer or store coupon, but the difference is easy to untangle if you know how to read barcodes. Barcodes are those long sections of black and white lines resting above a series of numbers. By looking at a coupon's barcode, you can easily tell if a coupon is actually a store or manufacturer coupon–and this can make all the difference in the world.

Look closely at this Clean & Clear® coupon. Is it a manufacturer or store coupon? Where and how can it be used? Well, the average person would think it is a manufacturer coupon because it says so right on the top. But it's not. Look more carefully. See that single barcode with the "**RC**" before the numbers? RC is Rite Aid®'s code for coupons, indicating that it is a store coupon. Yes, yes, I understand it says "Manufacturer's Coupon," but it isn't actually one. Any barcode coded with RC (Rite Aid® Coupon) is a store-only coupon. That means it can be combined with a manufacturer's coupon for greater savings. Clean & Clear® regularly offers coupons of up to $4.00 off its products, and if you were to use one of those true Clean & Clear® manufacturer coupons along with this example, you would likely get the item for free.

Now let's look at the two Target® examples: Both have the Target® symbol clearly displayed on them; one says "Target® Web Coupon," the other says "Manufacturer's Coupon." Which is which, and how do you use them? A single barcode almost always applies specifically to store coupons, so the top coupon must be a store coupon. We know it's not coded with a great indicator like RC to guide us, so we have to rely on the store symbol. Also, Target® explicitly writes out the company name on the web coupon. As for the bottom coupon, it doesn't say Target® on it, but certainly shows Target®'s logo. And although it does suggest that it should be used at Target® via the logo, it isn't restricted to Target® stores. You could use it anywhere. So, the top coupon is a store coupon and the bottom one is a manufacturer coupon.

In case you are still confused, you can always look for one single indicator above all else: the "Remit to Address," or the area noted for "Retailer." If a coupon has a note on it for the retailer to send the coupon to a manufacturer's address, or its parent company's address for reimbursement, then it is most certainly a manufacturer coupon and therefore can be used anywhere, except where explicitly written other-

wise. On the Aleve® coupon pictured here, it says, "Redeemable at Rite-Aid® Only" just under the incorpora-tion date.

Coupon Types

So far, most of the examples we have been using are item coupons. Although they are the most common, they are just one type of coupon. The other type is called a **transaction coupon (Trans Q or TQ)**. Every coupon is one of these two types. Item coupons relate to a specific item, and must be properly matched to brand, size, and any other particulars about the product specified on the coupon. As we have seen, both stores and manufacturers put out item-specific coupons. Transaction coupons are usually store coupons, but from time to time, a manufacturer may put one out. Transaction coupons are a certain dollar reduction or percentage off the top when the total pur-chase has reached the amount stated on the coupon. For example, if you bought $20 worth of items at CVS®, you would be able to take $5 off with one of its $5/$20 coupons.

Most transaction store coupons are issued by retailers other than grocery stores. Lowes® and Home Depot®, Old Navy® and Banana Republic®, Target®, Bath & Body Works®, Office Max®, Macy's®, and loads of other retailers use transaction coupons to encourage buyers. You probably won't find a transaction coupon in your supermarket flyer, but through a little effort, like signing up for store emails or mailing lists, or getting a store's loyalty card, you should be able to find plenty of them. Further, opening a store-issued credit card, particularly at department stores like Kohl's®, is a great way to get those 30% off and higher transaction coupons sent to you.

TOPPING OFF

Charlene was shopping at the Gap® and had a "Spend $75, save $10 off your Total" ($10/$75) coupon. She was holding a pair of jeans that cost $69.50. In order to save the ten dollars with her coupon, she had to buy more. The retailer hoped she would consider an extra item like a $22.50 camisole— the transaction coupon is intended to encourage just that sort of purchase. Unfortunately for the Gap®, Charlene was savvy enough to grab a pair of socks that cost only $6.50 rather than the cami, but you get the idea. By adding the $6.50 item, Charlene got free socks and saved an additional $3.50 on her jeans.

One kind of store that consistently utilizes TQs is drugstores. However, drugstores tend to offer a dollar amount off the transaction once the threshold is reached, rather than a percentage off. The amounts range considerably.

The most common include $3/$10, $4/$20, $5/$25, $6/$30, $10/$50, and $20/$100, just like this pictured $5/$25 Rite Aid® (RA) example:

Think of a transaction coupon this way. Coupons are a form of currency. You know the value of every bill you see in your wallet. However, would you try to spend these bills in the UK? Would you try using Indian rupees or Japanese yen in the States? Of course not, because you and the cashier would be working with two different currencies. Coupons

work exactly the same way—they are a form of payment. As a consumer, you need to know their value. Is it a store or manufacturer coupon, and how can it be combined? Is it an item or transaction coupon, and can it be combined? Knowing the specifics makes all the difference.

THREE ITEMS = SIX COUPONS!

Here I used three manufacturer's coupons, two each for Huggies® and one for the Motrin®. I also used three store coupons—one transaction coupon and two store item coupons good for diapers. By combining all six coupons on the three items, I saved over $20.00 on this purchase. Soon, you will be able to do the same!

Part II: The Stores

The second part of becoming an informed couponer involves the stores where you shop. To realize true savings, you need to know a store's coupon policy and the staff. Picking certain stores doesn't matter as much as knowing how the stores treat coupons. You can coupon successfully almost anywhere, but you need to know how to maximize the savings under that store's rules. Often a cashier won't know what the store's policy is, and if you have a firm understanding, you might be able to educate them—and save money in the process. Carry the store's policy with you until you've established a good relationship. That way, if there should be any dispute, you and the cashier both have the resources for a solution. Most cashiers, and certainly their managers, are thrilled to know how they should proceed. If you ever are rejected for coupon use and you happen to have the store policy with you, thereafter the staff will know you are honest and knowledgeable about coupons, and they will always accept what you give them. Be warned: there is a ton of fraud in the coupon world, and knowledge is the first step in separating yourself from the bad couponers.

Smart couponing starts with smart and honest couponers. Stores are plagued by unethical and fraudulent couponing, so you need to distinguish yourself from the con artists. Establishing relationships with the staff at your regular stores builds trust. Once the staff knows you personally, they trust your Qs as legitimate and, even better, may open registers just for you.

For example, some stores don't accept black and white coupons, because people fraudulently photocopy coupons. Never photocopy! If I could yell this from the rooftops I would, because unethical couponing hurts us all. Photocopying is not only completely unacceptable, it is a form of fraud. Though I think it is silly to worry about the color of printed coupons because people can just as easily photocopy in color as in black and white, it is important to be ethical every time so you can be known as an honest couponer. Color aside, the true difference is the relationship you establish with the cashier who takes your coupons. Because I know my cashiers and managers well and they trust me and my black-and-white coupons, I never have to waste my ink by printing in color. That wouldn't be very frugal of me, now would it?

Kindness is your most valuable asset because those who work in retail hear complaints all day from consumers, and eventually they turn a deaf ear. It is the friendly consumer whom they listen to, and remember. With regard to knowing your stores, I should also point out a solution to product or store problems: Customer Service. Call the store's national customer service if you have a problem because it is their job to resolve issues, not that of the people who work at the retail level. Skip the in-store management, which has lots of other things to deal with before they can get to you.

As a last resort, if you know you are couponing correctly and are getting nowhere with your cashier, just remember this rule: "If Denied, Don't Buy."

PRESSURE COOKER

Jacob shopped at a store where they didn't know him very well. He had many black-and-white coupons, each with distinct and authentic barcodes. The cashier refused to take most of his coupons, saying she thought they were fraudulent because he had copied them. Jake questioned her rationale, arguing that she had no reasonable premise for accepting only certain coupons. If the argument was that black and white meant photocopied, how were some okay but others were not? Jake wasn't pressured to buy because he kept to the "If Denied, Don't Buy" rule. He left the store and went elsewhere, where he bought his items and used all of those black-and-white coupons.

It's happened to me. Last winter I was shopping at a major chain store with which I am richly familiar, but I wasn't shopping at my regular store. My first mistake was assuming the neighboring store would trust me. But they didn't know who I was. Further, while the young cashier was having trouble ringing in a purchase for the lady in front of me, the acting supervisor stood behind the cashier. She was also on the phone discussing something very upsetting. I knew disaster was imminent and I was likely to get hit by her shrapnel. I should have just turned around and left but, against my better judgment, I instead strode up to the counter with $21.50 in products and $20.99 in black-and-white printed coupons. That poor flustered cashier just looked at my pile and shook his head. He proceeded to ask his supervisor what he should do. With just a quick glance, the manager pushed my coupons back across the counter, saying, "Too many—these look photocopied and we can't take them."

I calmly introduced myself by name. I told her that I actually teach couponing at a local college and that coupon ethics are extremely important to me. Since her store and my regular store are in the same district, I suggested she call over there. Well, she didn't care one bit and still refused to accept them. Although upset, I knew better than to buy those products at full price, so instead I left for my usual store in tears. The people there listened to my story, rang me up respectfully, and offered to call the district manager on my behalf, which I refused. The store manager actually gave me a hug! So you see, relationships can be so important to saving money.

More often than not, my couponing experiences have been excellent, and I cherish the people I've met while shopping, both as a couponing teacher and shopper. During one grocery trip, the cashier yelled out my overall savings to everyone around us. Another time, I was able to give a supermarket employee who worked at the deli counter and whose husband recently lost his job enough coupons for toiletries to get them through the next month. You'll find that store employees can be very helpful when they look up and see you: one of their loyal customers.

Shopping off hours when there are fewer customers in the store makes it easier to get to know the cashiers and other store staff. It's like stopping for gas or coffee on your way to work and regularly seeing the same employee each day. Workers at your favorite store tend to keep the same shift schedules, so try to set a regular shopping schedule so you can get familiar with cashiers to some degree. All relationships have to start somewhere, so make the effort!

DO YOU KNOW YOUR QS?

1. **What is a store coupon?**
   a. A transaction coupon to be used anywhere.
   b. A coupon for a specific item printed by its manufacturer.
   c. Any coupon produced by a store only for use there.

2. **A store coupon can be …**
   a. A transaction coupon.
   b. A coupon for a specific item.
   c. Either.

3. **Which is not a manufacturer coupon?**
   a. Any coupon produced by a store only for use there.
   b. A coupon for a specific item printed by its manufacturer.
   c. A transaction coupon to be used anywhere.

4. **A manufacturer coupon can be …**
   a. A transaction coupon only.
   b. A coupon for a specific item or a transaction coupon.
   c. A coupon for a specific item only.

5. **What are two ways to distinguish between store and manufacturer Qs?**
   a. Triple barcodes and remit-to addresses.
   b. Store logos and remit-to addresses.
   c. Triple barcodes and store logos.

6. Which abbreviation below represents a transaction coupon?

   a. $.50/1

   b. $5/$20

   c. $1/2

7. Which abbreviation below also represents a transaction coupon?

   a. $0.50 off one item

   b. 30% off any item

   c. 30% off entire purchase

8. Two important things to know about your stores are?

   a. Sales and staff.

   b. Coupon policy and sales.

   c. Staff and coupon policy.

9. Black and white printed coupons are?

   a. Unusable.

   b. Totally legitimate.

   c. Beyond my technological understanding.

10. What is your most valuable asset?

   a. BOGO sales

   b. Gift cards

   c. Kindness

Answers: 1. c, 2. c, 3. a, 4. b, 5. a, 6. b, 7. c, 8. c, 9. b, 10. c

CHAPTER 3

Finding Coupons

DO YOU THINK COUPONING MEANS TAKING out your scissors and spending hours on Sunday with newspaper flyers? Think again. I never cut coupons until a few minutes before I leave for the store. Even in that case, many of my coupons come ready-cut from the manufacturers themselves. I haven't the time, or the interest, to cramp my lazy little fingers with scissors. No, thank you. All I want my fingers wrapped around is the handle on my coffee mug. There is so much more to do on a Sunday than worry about keeping track of tiny scraps of perforated clippings.

Let me break down where to find the coupons you want so you don't have to do the work. Coupons come from a wide variety of sources, and though the search does start in newspapers, you certainly aren't limited to them. Coupons are found on the Internet, in stores, product samples, from manufacturer mailings, magazines, and libraries, just to name a few. You may not have noticed coupons that were sitting right there in front of you, because you didn't know where to look. How many times have you passed a Tear Pad or Blinkie? Those coupons were just begging you to take them and you just walked on by. From now on, you will walk past them no more. You'll pluck one off and say thank you very much. So let's get started!

Tucked Inside Your Newspaper

The first step in couponing is buying a Sunday paper. Most Sunday newspapers are loaded with lots of coupons and information relating to coupons. You may think that spending extra money is not the way to save money, but I promise you, you will easily recoup the cost of the paper. If you have the Sunday paper delivered, because you're not going to remember to buy it every week, make sure to ask for a special low rate for new subscribers or a match on a competitor's delivery price, if it isn't already advertised.

EXCUSE ME, DO YOU MIND?

You don't necessarily have to subscribe to newspapers to get the inserts. Ask your neighbors if they use their coupons; check with your local hotels, hospitals, nursing homes, or cafés to see if you can grab the inserts; look in office, condo, or apartment recycling bins; and check the local "free" papers because they usually include SmartSource inserts. Is the person ahead of you in line also buying a Sunday newspaper? Ask if he plans on using those Qs!

Once you get your paper, remove all your circulars and inserts, putting the inserts aside. Write the date on the outside cover of every insert you have, then file them away. Don't bother to look at the coupons until you're ready to go shopping. For now, sort them by insert type, date them, then stack them together for another time. Do NOT cut out the coupons.

In-Ad Coupons

When the time is right—right before you go shopping—you'll want to check all your sources. Inside the paper, you should look first at the store flyers. These are the advertised sales that stores send out as circulars. They are important because they include information about sales and special promotions, too. Flyers differ from inserts because flyers are the information about sales and sometimes contain coupons, while inserts are entirely made up of coupons and offer no sale information.

Coupons printed in the circulars or flyers are called **in-ad coupons (in-ad Qs)** and vary widely. In-ad coupons can be either strictly for use at the store that printed the circular or possibly a manufacturer's coupon to be used anywhere. They can also vary in type, such as item or transaction coupons. Sometimes, store flyers include specialty coupons called **Coupon Doublers**. When used along with traditional coupons, Doublers double the value for the coupons you're using.

A flyer's information about a sale or promotion can be very helpful when deciding where you are going to use your coupons. Suppose you planned to buy some Transformers for your nephew's birthday (approximately $6 each) and you have a Hasbro™ manufacturer coupon for $5/$25 Transformers toys. Wouldn't you like to know that Toys"R"Us® is offering a **Buy One Get Two (B1G2)** sale on Transformers? That way, rather than going to Walmart® and getting four Transformers for $24 as planned, you can go to Toys"R"Us and get 15 for the same price. That's right: 15! Then you can give your nephew 10, and donate the other five to Toys for Tots without any extra cost to you. And, since Toys"R"Us and Walmart® are only a stone's throw apart, you didn't waste your time driving around or your money on extra gas.

Coupon Inserts

Inserts are those pages of coupons that are nestled amongst the flyers. Inserts are not the flyers or adver- tised sales, but the actual coupon book- lets. There are three  main types of inserts: SmartSource®, RedPlum™, and Proc- tor & Gamble.

SmartSource is a regional insert that we couponers denote as **SS**, followed by the date it is released. Since SmartSource is distributed weekly, the insert for the week of November 21 would be filed as SS11/21. Many times, your Sunday newspaper will include two SmartSource® inserts, one thicker than the other. In that case, we refer to the thicker of the two as SS#1 and the thinner as SS#2

followed by dates in parentheses, such as SS#2(11/21). SmartSource® coupons are more grocery store–focused, and they cover, but aren't limited to, manufacturer coupons for items like Lysol®, Betty Crocker®, and Land O'Lakes®.

RedPlum issues the second weekly insert, though sometimes bi-weekly. RedPlum™ is abbreviated **RP** and followed by the date, such as RP11/21. The RedPlum™ insert is also a regional insert, and when a newspaper includes two, they are also abbreviated accordingly—RP#1(11/21) or RP#2(11/21). The RedPlum insert is focused more broadly than grocery stores. It supplies local coupons and deals for groceries, restaurants, home improvement, and personal care. The inserts include coupons for Hillshire Farm®, Newman's Own®, and L'Oréal®, to name a few. Because RedPlum™ is distributed by **Valassis**, on couponing blog sites sometimes you may see a **V**11/21 noted instead of RP11/21. Since both RedPlum™ and SmartSource® are regional inserts, sometimes the coupons differ slightly from one geographic area to another.

A third, and most impressive, source is the Proctor & Gamble Insert (P&G) because it generally has higher-value coupons within it. The P&G insert covers many of your regular non-food items, since Proctor & Gamble is the umbrella company for makers of pharmaceuticals, cleaning supplies, personal care items, and pet  supplies. The insert is usually distributed in the beginning of the month. In addition to the monthly distribution, P&G also publishes a second special insert that comes out seasonally in a mid-month Sunday newspaper. Also, while RedPlum™ and SmartSource® do not print inserts on major holiday weekends, the holidays do not affect Proctor & Gamble's timing, so be on the lookout. When your Sunday paper does include a P&G Insert, I suggest you buy two. The savings gained through P&G coupons will compensate for the cost of buying an extra paper because the coupons apply to typical items in most households.

Other inserts also pop up from time to time in the papers.

An important insert that doesn't appear on a weekly basis is the **General Mills Everyday Saver (GM)**. It is filled with coupons for GM products, and you should also purchase an extra newspaper when you see it included. Though General Mills publishes its own insert on occasion, it also releases coupons in the SmartSource® insert, especially for its brands like Betty Crocker®. Similarly, Unilever and Campbell's® sporadically send out inserts of their own, but more typically, they publish product coupons in one of the existing RedPlum™ or SmartSource® inserts. Expect to find quarterly publications of Unilever and Nestle® coupons in single issues of RedPlum® and Kellogg's® and Kraft® in SmartSource.

BUYING PAPERS

1. Buy the cheapest newspaper with inserts you can find when buying papers solely for the inserts, except check the inserts against those offered in the most expensive papers. Most times they'll be the same, but occasionally you'll have to buy the latter.
2. During holiday time or weeks including P&G or GM inserts, consider buying duplicate papers.
3. No matter which paper you buy, remember to check for all its inserts before you leave the store. You don't want to buy a paper without coupons!

While You're Shopping

You can also find coupons while you're shopping. Coupons can be found everywhere. Sometimes you'll find coupons that people have left on the shelf next to products. Other times the distributer will set up little machines. But you'll rarely find them if you don't look! Each time you shop, you should focus one eye on shopping and the other on coupon-hunting.

As soon as you enter the grocery store, begin to look for coupons. Many stores post coupons in the entryway along with advertisements, community classifieds, and unadvertised store sales. Look through brochures and free local papers you find there, too, as many brochures include coupons and rebates while the free papers might have full inserts. If your store has a section like this, be sure to check it out.

Another great place to check for coupons is the customer service desk. Some stores have stacks of coupons that shoppers totally ignore. I still can't believe that most shoppers don't bother to check this area out for coupons. I mean, I consider myself a lazy couponer, but walking by coupons while you're shopping is such a lost opportunity! Customer service areas usually have lots of manufacturer coupons and store coupons (if your store offers them) unless it has a separate designated coupon area. If you aren't sure where an area like that might be, just look for where your store keeps its weekly circular. The coupons are generally nearby.

Other in-store coupons are located near products throughout the store. They come in many different forms and you need to know what to look for. First, there are **Peelies**. Peelies are those annoying little sticker-like coupons stuck on product packages. Pictured on this Raisin Bran® box is a $1.00 Kellogg's® Peelies

for the cereal. I say annoying, because they always stick to my fingers when I try pulling them off. However, Peelies are worth a bit of aggravation since they are attached right to the items you want to buy! Is there anything easier?

Well, maybe. I think Blinkies are more exciting than Peelies because the little machine that dispenses them beckons me to it. Blinkies are coupons distributed from a machine that hangs on the shelf near the product for which the coupon can be used. The Blinkie machine is roughly boxed shaped and has a small green or red light that blinks when you walk by. The light is meant to attract your attention and thus gives the coupon its name. A coupon is usually sticking out, ready to pull when you pass, and if you take the coupon, the Blinkie machine then makes a little noise and spits out another Blinkie coupon, which you can also take. Should you take two coupons, the machine will slow its speed in printing out more. It is self-timed to adjust to the frequency of Blinkie coupons pulled, but if you are willing to wait, feel free to take as many as you can use.

Tags, or **Taggies**, are coupons found hanging on the items themselves. The first Taggies hung exclusively off beer and wine, and were thus called Beer and Wine Tags. Though you didn't necessarily have to purchase the alcohol, they began as a way to offer money off meat—poultry, seafood, and beef. The marketing idea is to encourage shoppers to purchase an alcoholic beverage to pair with the protein you were already buying. The tag or, more rarely called a **collar**, can also include discounts on flowers, ice, cheese, or nuts. Really, anything you might want to have along with a glass of wine or bottle of beer. Ironically, you rarely need to purchase the alcohol in order to use the coupon.

Most Beer and Wine Taggies never mention alcohol purchase requirements and broadly offer discounts for *any* brand. Because of state-to-state differences in liquor laws, restrictions and purchase requirements differ. Read every taggie you pull from alcohol bottles to check for rules like, "$2.00 off any meat purchase of $5.00 or more" or "must be used with purchase of wine and seafood" or "not valid in MA," for example. Nowadays, tags seem to hang on all kinds of products sold in jars or bottles. I've even seen a taggie hanging off a bottle of stool softener.

Tear Pads are yet another way to pick up coupons while
you are shopping in the
store. Tear Pads are pads
of coupons attached to a
cardboard advertisement
that also hang near the
items for which the
coupons can used. Some-
times Tear Pad coupons
are displayed on the
shelves within the aisles.

Here is an example of a Tear Pad for Finish® Quantumatic™
dishwasher detergent dispenser system that I found displayed in the aisle, hanging off the shelf. Other times, they
are attached to the front of display cases, end aisles, or
coolers. The dispensers attached to cooler displays, freezers, or refrigerators are sometimes called Freezer Extras.
Coupons in such brightly colored Freezer Extras relate to
the products behind the glass or in displayed in the cooler.

The last few places you can find coupons while in your
store are at sample tables, at some price-scanning
machines, or on the cash register tape at checkout. Sample tables are an excellent place to find coupons. If a manufacturer is willing to pay a person to stand there and hand
out samples, they usually have coupons available, too. If
you don't see any, just ask!

Also consider scanning your loyalty cards at places with
price scanners. CVS® is a perfect example of a chain that
offers coupons through its price scanners. Simply scan the
barcode on your CVS ExtraCare card where you would
normally line up the item barcode to check for the price.
Instead of giving you a price, the scanner will print out

card-driven coupons. Check the side of the machine.

Printouts at the end of your receipt, on the actual **cash register tape**, are called **CRTs**. The ExtraCare Bucks, Register Rewards, and UP Rewards obtained at CVS®, Walgreens, and Rite Aid® respectively, are all forms of CRTs. Any coupon printed on the back of your receipt is also considered a CRT.

The last coupon you can get at a grocery store is called a CAT, which is printed from the little machine next to the cash register and is usually handed to you along with your receipt. CATs will be covered in detail in Chapter 5 (page 101).

Mining the Internet

You can also get coupons online, but from far more sources than you may think, and it took me a long time to compile such a great list to share with you. Read it while you have a foot bath and glass of wine. You've earned the right just by reading this chapter and saving yourself all that time searching in the far reaches of the Web.

The Internet is a great resource for coupons. Once you find one on the Internet, you can print it out and use it just like coupons you find in newspaper inserts. While you can print coupons from many Internet sites, Coupons.com (www.coupons.com), SmartSource® (www.SmartSource.com), and RedPlum™ (www.redplum.com) are considered the main three. They work similarly by making many different manufacturer and store coupons available to you. With all three websites you will have to first log on to the site to see the coupons. Once you've entered the web address into the browser, coupon pictures will appear. A window will appear where you can place your zip code to see additional coupons. Check any of the coupons you want, then click the "print all selected coupons" button. (Do not click the "print all" button, or you'll waste both your paper and ink.) In order for the coupons to print, make sure you are hooked up to your printer and have already downloaded Java or any coupon printer software needed. If you haven't, the website will prompt you to do so. So all that's left is to remove the printed coupons from the printer and cut along the dotted edges. Then they are ready to use.

DOWNLOADING PRINTER SOFTWARE

Any time you download coupon printer software from the Internet, you should be aware that other stuff may be packed into the programming as well. Be wary of alternative sites or a downloading procedure that seems unusual, because you don't know what else might be loaded in the software package. If you have already started downloading, you can hit "cancel" to stop it. Major coupon sites, like Coupons.com, use downloadable coupon printer applets that prove worry free.

Coupon Database

As a couponer, your best online resources for finding coupons are the coupon databases. Just Google™ the words "coupon database" and pages of database links are at your fingertips. Since there are so many, you have to decide which you like best. I prefer coupon databases that do not require memberships to access, so I can limit the amount of information I share on the Internet. I also prefer those with few to no pop-up ads. Therefore, my favorite three **coupon databases (Qdb)** are hosted by **Deal Seeking Mom (DSM)**, **Krazy Coupon Lady (KCL)**, and **Hot Coupon World (HCW)**.

Deal Seeking Mom, run by an Ohio-based woman, is a wonderful coupon database (http://coupondatabase. dealseekingmom.com/main-database/) where you can enter a product by name, manufacturer, or type in the search bar, and an organized list of related coupons will pop up. The coupons are sorted into the following fields: description, value, expiration, source, limitations, store, and blogging format, making it very easy to determine which coupons will best work for you. For example, if I entered the word "oatmeal" into the search bar, I might get a list of nine oatmeal coupons consisting of five different manufacturers and six different sources, three of which are accessible by clicking the posted link. However, if I were to enter Bob's Red Mill® Oats, I'd be limited to that manufacturer and only two sources, both available in newspaper inserts.

The Krazy Coupon Lady's Q database is run by two women from California and Idaho. They present an alphabetized list of printable coupon links that is constantly updated and maintained. The beauty of this site is that every coupon is an Internet printable or a link to the Internet printable. So if you haven't bought Sunday's paper or subscribed to a particular magazine, for example, you don't have to worry about missing out on a coupon because KCL's Q database will pull together only the printable coupons (http://thekrazycouponlady.com/print-coupons/).

Hot Coupon World is the final database I want to mention. HCW is a community forum whose main coupon database (http://www.hotcouponworld.com/forums/coupon.php) is set up like Deal Seeking Mom's search field, but offers more flexibility in sorting the information gathered. HCW's database permits you to search and sort by description, value, source, store, category, or expiration date. It also allows you to set search limitations.

Sometimes Internet printables are available by clicking on links found on couponing blogs or forums. Couponing blogs or forums are websites that specialize in coupons and deals and some are maintained primarily by the hosting party, like DSM or KCL, while others contain more user-supplied information, like the websites from HCW or How to Shop for Free (www.howtoshopforfree.net). Others, for example, like the iheart sites (www.iheartcvs.com, www.iheartwags.com, www.iheartriteaid.com) list deals with corresponding coupon links to maximize savings.

Finding coupons through couponing blogs and link sites is as easy as clicking the link and printing. Sometimes you will need to fill out an information form to first access the coupon. Other times you'll print through your downloaded coupon printer app, and sometimes you'll be linked to a Brick's coupon, like the one pictured for A+D® diaper cream. In order to print a Brick's coupon twice, you can't just hit the back button and reprint because sometimes the information resubmitted triggers the coupon to think you're overprinting.

To be safe, use the drop-down arrow next to the back button and highlight the "Print Your Coupon" field. It will bring you back to the original screen from where you can click and print again!

```
  A+D® – Diaper Rash
  S Coupon Print
  S Coupon Print
  S Coupon Print
✓ Print Your Coupon
```

```
  S Coupon Print
✓ Print Your Coupon
```

Manufacturer Websites

Many manufacturer websites have links to coupons as well.
Before you leave to go shopping, take a second to check a
coupon's manufacturer's (manu) website. For example, if I
wanted to purchase Listerine® and didn't
have a coupon, I would pop on to the Lis-
terine website (www.listerine.com) before
I left for the store. By doing that, I would
be able to access three different $1.00/1
Listerine® coupons. You are very likely to
find coupons on a manufacturer's website.
Simply click the "Coupons" or "Special
Offers" tab, which will give you a list of
coupons available for those products.
Sometimes, saving money is just that easy.
   Another thing to consider while on the

manufacturer websites is to sign up for email newsletters. Most manufacturers send out loyalty coupons to those on their e-mailing lists. Try emailing the manufacturers, too. Directly contacting manufacturers is almost always good for a coupon or two. Manufacturers love to hear about how much you love their product, and they compensate you for your time by sending you a coupon as thanks. Computers not your thing? Call or write to the manufacturers. They respond just as well by old-fashioned methods as by email. You can also ask to be on traditional mailing lists to get those extra coupons, too.

Store Websites

Stores also make coupons available on their websites. To access coupons for some stores, all you need to do is go to their websites. Whole Foods® (www.wholefoodsmarket.com/coupons/) and Target® (http://coupons.target.com) are two stores that make finding coupons very easy. The websites are set up similarly to Coupons.com and Smart-Source.com®, so all you need to do is check the coupons you want and then print. CVS®, through CVS Savings Central (http://cvs.triaddigital.com), looks more like a manufacturer's website in that you must first click the "In-Store Coupons" tab before you can click each coupon to print.

Other sites, like that of New England grocery chain Shaw's® Supermarkets (http://info.shaws.com/coupons) require you to download a PDF of the coupons. The PDF looks like a page of coupons you would find in an insert, and you must cut out those you want.

Like Rite Aid®, other stores also offer online accessible coupons, but through a slightly more complicated system. Rite Aid® Video Values coupons are downloadable to print after you watch a video for the products. Offered through

the AdPerk website, the Rite Aid® coupons obtained through this system are referred to as AdPerk, **Video Values (VV)** or **Rite Aid (RA)** Qs. By logging on to AdPerk (http://my.AdPerk.com), you pick the product video you want to watch. The bottom right-hand side of the status bar tells you how long it is (usually 15 seconds to two min-

utes), and when it is done playing, a security code will appear in the center. You have thirty seconds to enter the code, accessing the coupon. From there you click the "My Rewards" bar, check off the "Select to Print" boxes for the coupons you want, then hit "Print Coupons."

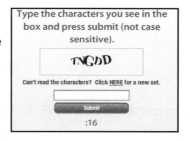

Facebook

Another great Internet source for finding coupons is Facebook®. Both manufacturers, such as Food Should Taste Good® all-natural chips, and stores, like Lowes® Home Improvement, offer coupons through Facebook.

Liking the Facebook link is usually good for a coupon or two, but during holiday give-a-ways, like that offered by Lowes, you might get many coupons, including some up to 90% off.

Old Navy® uses Facebook in a completely original way for earning coupons, as it allows Old Navy fans to play little games like Barker's Bones. Each week a new coupon is "buried" in one of the holes and you must find the coupon by clicking the holes to "dig it up." Once you find the right hole, a coupon pops up that you can either print immediately or have sent to your email address.

Smart Phones & E-Coupons

Modern technology is reinventing the coupon world, and now coupons can be loaded on to your loyalty cards and smart phones. What could be easier than having a cashier scan your phone for extra discounts?

E-Coupons, which are the coupons sent to the loyalty cards, are stored directly on the card. If you want to save $1.00 on two bags of Hershey's® Kisses, all you have to do is load your card with the coupon. Later, at your point of purchase, the coupon is automatically applied when the cashier scans your card. Websites like Cellfire.com make this process easy. By signing up for these free sites, you can use your computer to browse through all the available e-coupons and choose those you want. Once you select the coupons and enter your loyalty card number, you are ready to go. Not all grocery loyalty cards are loadable for e-coupons, so you'll have to check your store or the sites like Cellfire. For example, you can download e-coupons to Randall's, Smith's®, Kroger®, Vons®, Fred Meyer®, Shop Rite®, King Soopers®, and Ralphs® loyalty cards, but not with Stop & Shop®, Johnny's, or Shaw's® loyalty cards.

While your store can decide whether to make loadable e-coupons available to shoppers or not, you still have the option to use your smart phone for e-coupons. If you have a smart phone like an iPhone or Blackberry, you can pretty much do the same thing. In fact, Cellfire offers great deals on shopping, restaurants, and more, even tailoring the coupons to what can be used in your area. You can load coupons on your phone with codes to show the cashier or coupons with actual barcodes ready to scan. Just show her the phone and she can zap it with the scan gun and record your discount.

Tech-savvy retailers, like the Gap®, make couponing with your cell one step easier, by accessing the Internet and utilizing Facebook. Gap just ran a mobile phone deal for a free pair of jeans. First you had to login to Facebook®, then go to the Facebook Places App. And once you went to the store, you had to check in on Facebook. A

pop-up window telling you about the event appeared on your cell. All you had to do was click "claim" and find an employee to whom you could show your phone for a free pair of jeans or 40% off one item. Now that's easy couponing!

Virtual Coupons

The coupons we've discussed so far finding on the Web have been Internet printables, or coupons you print. But you can also take advantage of another type of coupons called online coupon codes. These are the online codes you must enter to get discounts for an Internet order. For example, if you are ordering a book online from Barnes & Noble® (www.BN.com), you would want to use a coupon code on the order. Coupon codes are series of numbers and letters that you must enter at checkout, like **8SAMPLE8**, after which the discount will be applied to a single item or multiple items in your cart. Sometimes online coupon codes work like transaction coupons. Entering the code discounts the total by a set dollar amount or percentage.

Finding online codes is even easier than finding Internet printables. If you regularly shop at an online store, join its emailing list. Also, once you order from a store online, they generally will send you a courtesy coupon code for your next order with them. However, should you still not have a coupon code and are at the online checkout, open up another window in your browser and visit the RetailMeNot site (www.retailmenot.com). For example, let's pretend you are making that order at Barnes & Noble® and have no coupon code. Type "BN.com" into the search bar at RetailMeNot. Click the search button and a list of applicable codes comes up. To get the discount, simply cut and paste the code from there to the Barnes & Noble coupon box on the payment screen.

Alternatively, you can also click any coupon code displayed on the RetailMeNot list, and it will copy and open the shopping site with the coupon code already applied to your shopping cart.

Auction Sites

Finally, in discussing where to find coupons on the Internet, we need to talk about eBay® (www.eBay.com) and E-junkie (www.e-junkie.com). Both sites work similarly in that you can find available coupons by typing what you need into the search bar. At E-junkie, for example, if I were to search for Kohl's® coupons, I would type "Kohls" into the search field and change the drop-down arrow next to it to "Marketplace" before clicking the search tab. You'll find many choices of coupons available. However, it's up to you to decide whether buying the coupons is ethical (see more on this topic in Playing by the Rules, page 196).

BUYER BEWARE

If a coupon value you find on an Internet source, especially eBay®, seems too good to be true, it probably is. Be especially wary of free-item or full-value Qs. If the picture looks strange, don't get it. If you do get some, check the coupons for raised print or shiny emblems to verify their authenticity before using. If you are still unsure, don't use them, and report the seller to eBay®!

If you look for coupons on eBay, you'll need to be more specific. For example, entering the word "coupon" into the search field yielded me 55,000 results. The better approach is to search by store or manufacturer name or by searching "restaurant coupons." You can also specify a particular type of coupon, such as entering "free coupons" or "BOGO" into the search field; that will give you over

8,000 results. Also, whole inserts are available on eBay. Type "RedPlum," "SmartSource," "P&G®" or just "coupon inserts," and see what exists. When getting coupons on sites like eBay® or E-junkie, you must understand that you are not bidding on or paying for the actual coupons, but the handling time it takes the person to put them together and ship them off to you. Coupons cannot be sold or bought.

Samples

I believe the best coupons are those you get directly from manufacturers, and the best of all come in product samples. You can get product samples from signing up for promotional or new product launch mailing lists on manufacturer websites, or by writing or calling companies and asking to be added to such lists. Also, you can get sample packages from accessing sources through Walmart® (http://instoresnow.walmart.com) and MySavings (http://mysavings.com) by clicking on the free sample link or by searching websites like the Freebie Blogger (http://thefreebieblogger.com/) that are dedicated to listing available free samples. You can sign up for the P&GbrandSampler, where you get product samples offered by Proctor & Gamble through www.pgeveryday solutions.com.

You can also join programs dedicated to sending out samples in order to solicit consumer response or reviews, like Vocalpoint (www.vocalpoint.com), which uses a "Trys and Tells" system to send out samples and coupons, after which you are expected to answer surveys about the product. Expo (www.expotv.com) features a "Tryology" system and hopes you'll upload video reviews of samples you've received. Pictured is my Kashi® sample from Vocal that came with six coupons, one for $3.00 off my next purchase.

The best coupons and samples come from taking part in programs where you host product parties. PSSST by General Mills (http://pssst.general mills.com) provides hosting opportunities featuring GM products through its MyGetTogether program. Houseparty (www.house-party.com) works similarly to the GM program, extending hosting opportunities for

product-based parties, though it includes a variety of products from many manufacturers. Should you be selected by either program, you agree to host a party in your home, office, etc., based around the product promotion or theme. Invite friends, family or coworkers, and you'll receive a box of goodies that always includes samples and coupons, among other theme-based gifts.

Afterward, just write about your party experience, upload a picture or two, and you and your guests can keep the coupons. My mother-in-law is pictured here holding the coupons and treats she got as a guest of a Houseparty I hosted featuring Arnold® Sandwich Thins.

Alternative Sources

You can discover many alternative sources for coupons that until now you may not have considered, such as doctors' offices. Your child's pediatrician, for

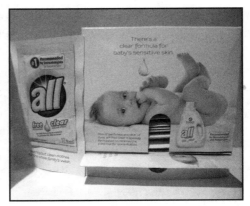

instance, is likely to receive samples or coupons for kid-friendly medicines, diaper products, or even gentle detergent. This pictured All® sample was displayed on the office counter at my sons' pediatrician, Dr. Alice Merkrebs. Your dentist likely has toothpaste, aspirin, or even sugar-free gum coupons, and your chiropractor could have body balms and ThermaCare® Qs. Some of those fine practitioners leave samples and coupons in their waiting rooms, while you may have to ask for others. What else are you going to do before your name is called, read half a magazine article?

Speaking of magazines, they can be wonderful coupon sources. Almost every kind of magazine contains coupons, should you bother to look. In men's magazines such as *Maxim*, you will find coupons for a product like Dove® Men + Care Body Wash, while in *Marie Claire* you might find Maybelline Color Sensational® Lipcolor coupons. The coupons found in magazines relate to the target® reader, so keep that in mind when searching for Qs. Even trade magazines sometimes offer interest-specific coupons to their readers. Any magazine marketed to crafty women or stay-at-home moms, like *Good Housekeeping*, *Country Living*, *Parents*, or *Parenting Magazine*, is going to have more coupons in general, because the women who read them typically do most of the household shopping. If you want a magazine loaded with coupons, you'll want to order a subscription to *All You* magazine.

This monthly magazine can be purchased exclusively at Walmart® retailers, but it is also available by subscription. *All You* magazine **(AY)** is filled with  coupons, like the $81.55 in coupons of this issue, and almost always pays for itself and more in return.

Finally, consider your friends, co-workers, and family as untapped coupon sources. Begin trading coupons at work or start a coupon chain where you can trade coupons by mail. All coupon chains are different, some may be for solely baby items or organic foods; others may be restricted to grocery coupons or cover any product or store. Q chains can be started by anyone, but whoever starts the chain decides the rules. Typically, coupon chains follow a mailing list and those who pull from the coupons must replace them.

COUPON CHAIN ETIQUETTE

1. Send great coupons and you will get great coupons.
2. Try to include at least one free item, high value or BOGO Q.
3. Strictly follow the mail-to order so that no one is accidentally skipped.
4. Always check the order before sending to see if it has changed. People move, quit, or go on vacation, and you don't want to be the one to mess up your group's chain.

Check your local library or church for coupons. If they don't already have one, set up a coupon exchange box. Did you recently move? Go to the post office and ask for a movers' coupon package. Are you a member of a social group, mothers' club, or other network? Tap that group for coupons and see what you'll get and give in the process.

Now that you know where to get coupons, you need to collect only the right ones. Focus on coupons for items you currently use, so you don't waste time clipping or printing everything in sight. Over-printing is a common mistake of newcomers to couponing, a trap in which I was entangled myself. Once you concentrate on looking for only what you need, you will save on ink cartridges and tired wrists as well.

You will also have to learn how to use coupons before printing them out. For example, is a $0.75 or $1.00 coupon worth more? Well, the answer depends on where you shop. Do you need to print daily, weekly, or monthly? How can you combine the coupons you have? What do you do with unused coupons? When you clip your coupons, you'll need to take all of these factors into consideration. The next chapter explores how to use your coupons to get the greatest savings possible on every shopping trip.

YOUR MONEY-SAVING JOURNEY HAS BEGUN

1. Where can you find in-ad coupons?
   a. Internet sources.
   b. Flyers.
   c. Inserts.

2. What are the three most common inserts?
   a. SmartSource®, Red Plum™, and General Mills.
   b. SmartSource®, General Mills, and P&G.
   c. P&G, SmartSource®, and Red Plum™.

3. Which of these coupon types are not found in stores?
   a. Taggies
   b. E-coupons
   c. Peelies

4. What do you call the in-store coupons found in the little square dispensers?
   a. Blinkies
   b. Peelies
   c. Taggies

5. Which store website utilizes Video Values or AdPerk for its coupons?
   a. Target®
   b. Shaw's®
   c. Rite Aid®

6. Internet coupons to be used shopping on the web are called ...

    a. E-coupons

    b. Coupon codes

    c. Downloadable coupons

7. Cellfire cannot help you load coupons to your ...

    a. Library card.

    b. Grocery loyalty card.

    c. Smart phone.

8. Which of these is not an example of a party-hosting program for coupons?

    a. House party.

    b. Cellfire.

    c. General Mills' MyGetTogether.

9. What should you set up at work, church, or at your library?

    a. Coupon Clubs.

    b. Coupon exchange boxes.

    c. Extra computers for printing coupons.

10. The best possible magazine source for coupons is ...

    a. *Redbook.*

    b. *Good Housekeeping.*

    c. *All You.*

Answers: 1. b, 2. c, 3. b, 4. a, 5. c, 6. b, 7. a, 8. b, 9. b, 10. c

CHAPTER 4

Using Coupons

NOW YOU KNOW ALL ABOUT COUPONS, WHERE to find them, and how to read them. All that's left is learning how to use them. Once you learn scenario-building, you can design shopping runs that actually pay for your basics and other desired products. Scenario-building can be done through many different combinations of the following: stacking, double coupons, overages, full-value coupons, BOGOs (buy one get ones), and even using expired coupons. Catalinas can also influence your scenarios, but we'll discuss those in detail in the next chapter. For now, let's get to work on some couponing magic.

You probably know how most people use coupons. They get their Sunday papers and pull out the inserts inside. Flipping through the inserts, they may cut out some coupons for products they like. Then they bring the coupons along with them to shop at the grocery store. That's it; they never even consider using coupons at other places where they shop! Maybe you are the same. Sometimes you buy an item because it is on sale and you have a matching coupon, but you've never thought out a plan beyond that. You didn't realize that the coupon policy at the store where you are shopping is as important as the prices themselves. So remember: your choice of store matters. It's your first step.

Second, it is extremely important to make a list. When you make lists, you (1) tend not to buy on impulse and (2) become more aware of the prices of the products you regularly purchase. By becoming familiar with your buying needs, you will spot more specials and sales that might be of interest to you. Overall, you'll be more aware when a deal is particularly good. When you see sales for products you like, you can go online to check the coupon databases for corresponding Qs (coupons). Then you can stack them all together and achieve much greater savings than the average Sunday clipper.

The key to scenario-building is to follow these easy steps:

1. Pick a store.
2. Make a list.
3. Note the specials (Advertised Sales/Dollar Threshold/Catalinas/etc.).
4. Check the coupon databases.
5. STACK, STACK, STACK!

The Art of Stacking

Stacking is the process by which you either combine store and manufacturer coupons, or transaction and item coupons, or any combination of the four. Stacking coupons is how you really rack up the savings.

KNOW YOUR STORE!

Looking through the inserts, Sheila sees a coupon for $0.75 off two jars of Skippy® peanut butter. She cuts the Q and buys the two jars of Skippy at $2.59 each. Using her coupon, she paid a total of $4.43. Sheila lives in Illinois and shops at Meijer®. Could she have done better by simply knowing her store?

Yes! Sheila could have saved more money several different ways at the very same store. First, Meijer was offering a coupon of $1.00 off three jars of Peter Pan® on its website. By downloading the online store coupon and substituting Peter Pan ($1.80 sale price) for Skippy, she would have paid a total of only $4.40 and gained an extra jar of peanut butter. Even if Sheila's kids will only eat Skippy peanut butter, she still could have saved more money. Her Meijer grocery store accepts both store and competitor's coupons. Sheila could have downloaded the $0.75 off two (.75/2) Skippy peanut butter coupon from Target® and used it along with her original Skippy manufacturer's Q, saving an additional $0.75 and bringing her total down to $3.68!

Step 1. Pick a Store

Decide where you want to shop before you worry about the rest of the process. While the general principles of stacking apply to any store you choose, each store offers variations in its specials or sales. Are the items you want on sale? What are the prices? Does the store take coupons? What's the store's coupon policy? For example, if you are at a store where they double (or triple) coupons, then the face value of the coupon should be doubled (or tripled). Should your chosen store accept transaction coupons, you'll want to plan for any fillers you need to reach the transaction total. Also, what if the store you chose produces store coupons? Wouldn't you want to see if you could get any to match-up with your manufacturer coupons? Yes, of course! These are all reasons to consider first where you are shopping.

Step 2. Make a List

"Make a list, check it twice, you're gonna find out what's the pricey price." (Okay, I am lame, but my point is this: making lists helps you learn your prices.) By making a list of the items you want to buy, you prepare yourself in several ways. First, you learn the prices of items you regularly buy and begin to realize when a deal is good or not. Second, you limit the number of impulse items you'll buy by putting your actual needs down on paper. Third, you won't tend to be conned into overbuying or stockpiling because some product on sale at the end of the aisle seems like a good deal. And, finally, making lists makes the process of checking the coupon databases for matching Qs (coupons) much easier.

Step 3. Note the Specials

Does a sale match up with your product(s)? Can you use a Trans Q (transaction coupon)? Are you combining store and manufacturer coupons? How you combine any of these specials will affect how you stack the coupons.

Step 4. Check the Coupon Databases

This is the easiest part of all. Turn on your computer, click open your Internet connection, and plug your favorite coupon database into the browser. My favorite is Deal Seeking Mom (http://coupondatabase.dealseekingmom.com), because all you have to do is enter an item in the search bar and the database will tell you where to get the coupon. If the existing coupon is in an insert, it will tell you which one, and you can refer to your filed inserts to find the coupon. If the coupon is available through a website, the database will provide the link: just click and print. Deal Seeking Mom is well organized, frequently updated, and easy to use. So, pop in the items on your list one at a time into the search bar to find where those coupons are. After, check the Qs (coupons) you picked up here and there over time and filed away. It's that easy. Now let's get to stacking.

Step 5. STACK, STACK, STACK!

This is the fun part, because now you gather together all the coupons you collected and head over to your store. The art of stacking is the process by which you combine all usable coupons, such as both manufacturer and store Qs (coupons), transaction and item Qs, and any specialty Qs that also apply.

Let's take a relatively easy example. Suppose you want to buy Prevacid®, a heartburn medication, which is on sale at CVS for $18.99. Being a smart shopper, you know that the regular price for a 24-count box of Prevacid is $21.99 and you think you can do better than the $3.00 off they offer. So you get your coupons together and build your scenario. Here's an example of how to go about it.

> **Step 1.** Pick a store. In this case, it's CVS, because you know the item is on sale, and since you have taken the time to learn the store policy, you also know that stacking both store and manufacturer coupons is allowed.

> **Step 2.** Make a list. You already know you want Prevacid at the $18.99 sale price. What else do you want?
> **Step 3.** Note the specials. Let's say you have a CVS® transaction coupon at $$5/$20 ($5 off with a $20 purchase). That means you need to bring your total

purchase to $20.00 to maximize your savings. There-fore, you must add a filler item that equals $1.01 or more to reach the $20 threshold. So, choose a $1.50 newspaper as a filler, and as a bonus you wind up getting even more coupons in the process. The use of the transaction coupon gave you $3.50 toward your purchase and additionally paid for all your new coupon inserts! Also, you've read the flyer and know Prevacid® earns $4 in ExtraCare Bucks (ECBs), which means that CVS will give you $4 back in ECBs—cash register tape printouts used like cash at CVS—bringing your actual cost down another $4.00. Combine that with a $6.00 CVS Prevacid store coupon you have on hand, and check for any other possible Qs (coupons) on the database.

Step 4. Check the coupon databases. Enter the word "Prevacid" in an online coupon database. It shows a $6/1 ($6 off one product) Prevacid®24HR manufacturer coupon available in the SmartSource® insert, dated for easy find. It will also list an expiration date for the coupon, so make sure you use it in time. Now go to your insert and clip!

Step 5. STACKING. Buy Prevacid®24HR, $18.99 and newspaper, $1.50 and follow the process below:
$20.49 ($18.99 Prevacid + $1.50 newspaper)
Transaction & Item Coupons (total above $20) use:
–$5/$20 CVS Transaction coupon
Store & Manufacturer Coupons Use:
–$6/1 Prevacid ®24HR Manufacturer coupon
–$6/1 Prevacid CVS coupon
Subtotal:

$3.49 Out of pocket (OOP)
–$4.00 in earned ExtraCare Bucks (ECBs)
= +$0.51 Money Maker (MM)

Good job. Not only did you save more than $3.00, but you actually made $0.51 on the deal and got your paper, too. How smart! Not so hard, right? I say, "Good for you!" It really doesn't matter so much where you shop, nor what you buy, but rather how you go about buying it.

In the Prevacid example, we stacked only three coupons against a sale, with a bonus that it was a CVS sale that included ECBs (ExtraCare Bucks). We did well, but overall it was a minor stacking example, as we bought only two items. Now let's look at a slightly more complicated example, using the same kinds of coupons but with an SCR (Single Check Rebate) entry at the end.

I buy a lot of diapers. Lots of diapers! With two- and three-year-old boys, I feel like I am surrounded by diapers, training pants, wipes, and dirty bums. While my oldest son is potty trained, he still wears Pull-Ups® at night. His younger brother is still in full-on diaper use, and only Huggies® Pure & Natural work for his sensitive skin. Therefore, I am compelled to know Huggies' costs and where and when to buy them. In this case, they are $8.99, and I'll buy them at Rite Aid®.

Follow this typical diaper scenario:
   Huggies @ Rite Aid® (RA)
   $17.98 (2) Huggies® Pure & Natural (P&N) diapers
   $2.99 (1) Johnson & Johnson (J&J) baby wash
   $20.97 subtotal
   –$5/$20 Rite Aid® Transaction Coupon
   –$4.00 (2) $2 Huggies Video Values (VV) Store
      Coupon

-$6.00 (2) $3 Huggies Manufacturer Coupon
-$1.00 Johnson & Johnson Video Values Store Coupon
-$1.00 Johnson & Johnson Manufacturer Coupon
$3.97 Out of Pocket (OOP)
-$3.99 Single Check Rebate (SCR) earning products
= +$.02 Money Maker

Okay, let's review the process that got us to making money rather than spending it:

Step 1. Pick a store. Because the drugstore policy allows stacking of Video Values, Store in-ad, and Manufacturer Coupons, Rite Aid® is the place where I prefer to buy diapers.

Step 2. Make a list. Huggies® Pure & Natural $8.99 each (sale price)–the list should focus on the items you want. The next step will round out the transaction.

Step 3. Note the specials. Video Values (Rite Aid® internal coupons earned watching videos) can be applied to both Huggies and Johnson & Johnson products. Also, I have a $5/$20 transaction coupon, so in this step I have to add to my desired items in order to reach the $20 threshold. The step can also be important for picking out items you may want but don't regularly buy.

Step 4. Check the coupon database. This will show you $3/1 Huggies® Pure & Natural on coupons.com, and a manufacturer website link for $1/1 Johnson & Johnson product. Print two of the Huggies coupons and the

Johnson & Johnson coupons. (I'd prefer to print more, but 2 is the maximum allowed.) Always check the data-bases for every item you intend to purchase.

Step 5. STACK, STACK, STACK!
Buy two Huggies, $17.98, and a Johnson & Johnson product, $2.99

We needed to purchase the Johnson & Johnson baby wash to hike the total over $20. That way we could use the $5/$20 transactional coupon. The baby wash was on sale for $2.99, and I found two separate coupons (store and manufacturer coupons) each for $1.00. Using the coupons brought the cost of the baby wash down to only $1.00. And since using it as the filler enabled us to use the $5/$20 transaction coupon, purchasing the Johnson & Johnson product actually produced a $4.00 gain. The $4.00 gain increased our savings on the diapers, much like overage on a product, bringing our total to $3.97.

Now, though I rarely bother with **mail-in-rebates (MIR)** because of my laziness, I always enter online my Rite Aid® receipts—store number, transaction number, and date of purchase into Rite Aid®'s **Single Check Rebate (SCR)** sys-tem. Single Check Rebates are actual checks that Rite Aid® mails you for buying products there. In this case, both the Huggies® and Johnson & Johnson products were qualify-ing items, at $3.00 and $.99 respectively. So we have already lowered the roughly $28 pre-sale cost to $3.97 out of pocket, and since Rite Aid® is sending along a check for $3.99, that brings our overall total to negative two cents! Yes, the store ended up paying us for the baby wash and packs of diapers.

Now that you understand the process of combining multiple coupons on single items, you are probably eager to learn about other types of coupons out there. These specialty coupons, and a store's doubling or tripling policies that make regular coupons special, can create even more advanced scenarios. Let's discuss a few.

Double Up

Do you know if your store doubles the value of your coupons? Many stores do! (Some stores even triple coupon values, though less commonly.) Generally speaking, stores won't double coupons worth $1 or more. When a store offers a coupon-doubling program, coupon values usually double from $.01–$.99 to $.02–$1.98. We already saw before how a $0.75 coupon could have a greater potential value than a $1.00 coupon, because the $0.75 doubled is worth $1.50. A handful of stores across the country, like Kroger® and Shaw's® Supermarkets double coupons every day, but most limit doubling to special promotions.

During these promotional weeks, stores also may issue special in-ad coupons called "Coupon Doublers": store-issued coupons that can be used to double the face value of regular coupons used with them. For instance, the grocery chain Albertsons®, which calls their doublers "Twice

Value Coupons," and the grocery chain Stop & Shop® both distribute $1.00 doublers from time to time in their flyers. Safeway sometimes distributes doublers up to a value of $0.50. Even if your grocer doubles coupons on a regular basis, as do Kroger® and Shaw's®

Supermarkets, continue to look for higher-value doublers they may offer. Shaw's, which always doubles coupons $0.99 or less in value, recently sent out $1.00 doublers in newspaper flyers and mailed-to-home flyers as a bonus to customers. You just never know.

Other times a store may limit doubling during a promotion period of a few days to a week. Still other stores choose to double only a limited number of coupons per transaction. For example, Kmart® recently offered a limited doubling campaign for anyone using Kmart®'s Loyalty Card. They restricted the doubling promotion to ten coupons per transaction. Yet the campaign included doubling $2.00 coupons up to $4.00 value! So, if you started with ten $2.00 coupons, the promotion resulted in an additional $20.00 in doubled-coupon savings (10 Qs x $2 = $20). If you live near a Kmart, watch for doubling campaigns because they are not offered often. Also, take advantage quickly, because once a special promotion is released to the general public, it can be pulled when a certain set number of people take advantage of the offer.

Sadly, doubling coupons is another area where fraudulent coupon use is plentiful, and is yet another reason why those relationships I earlier advised you to cultivate are so important.

If a coupon says DND, or more explicitly "Do Not Double," then the cashier is supposed to manually override the automatic doubling. Some cashiers do miss this, however, so it is your responsibility to point it out. Also, it is especially unethical to take any DND coupons to a self-checkout aisle in the hopes that the machine automatically doubles the value. While updated stores use "smart registers," capable of reading codes and automatically knowing whether a coupon can be doubled when scanned, not all stores have the technology. So don't ever knowingly take a Do Not Double coupon through the line where coupons are doubled.

DOUBLING RULES

Doublers—or Twice the Value Coupons—can absolutely be combined with DND (Do Not Double) manufacturer coupons unless the Doubler specifically states otherwise. The doubling coupon is a specialty coupon distributed by the store, which absorbs the loss when the coupons are used. This type of sale has nothing to do with the manufacturer. Since the manufacturer doesn't have to reimburse the store for the doubled-value of the coupon, the DND coding is unrelated to Doubler use.

DND—or Do Not Double—refers to use in traditional doubling stores that choose to double many coupons daily. You'll notice that DND is mostly written on coupons found within the stores, like in Blinkies or Taggies or Peelies. The manufacturer encodes the coupon as a DND so the doubling stores are still willing to offer them along side products without fear of revenue loss.

Therefore, coupons marked DND or explicitly Do Not Double can be used together with Doublers, but won't be doubled in regular doubling stores.

Reaching Your Limit

"Overage" is another aspect of couponing you must understand in order to maximize your couponing skills. An overage occurs when the coupon(s) you use for an item(s) is greater in value than the cost of the item itself. If you are lucky enough to shop a store that allows overages, the additional savings can be applied to other items in the transaction, but will not be given back to you in cash. Still, the extra saving is transferred to your other items, and the extra money is a wonderful little gain!

SHAKE YOUR MONEY MAKER

A Proctor & Gamble insert had a $5.00 coupon for "Select Olay® Products (Bar, Body Wash, In-Shower Body Lotion, and Body Lotion) **when you buy (WYB)** Secret® deodorant." Since the coupon had no size or quantity restrictions, savvy shoppers headed right over to an overage permitting store, where they purchased a trial size Secret® deodorant for $0.97 and a two-pack of Olay® bar soap for $2.49, totaling $3.46. With use of the $5.00 P&G coupon, they averaged $1.54 overage per set. While the store did not refund the $1.54 gain, it did allow the difference to be subtracted from the costs of other items purchased. It's like the shoppers were paid to shop!

Many cashiers are confused when dealing with an over-age, and when you are first starting out, sometimes you will find the value of coupons is denied when it causes an overage. The problem is easily resolved if you are an informed shopper.

Most commonly, overage occurs when you stack a store coupon and a manufacturer coupon and they exceed the value of the item you are purchasing. Since manufacturers don't reimburse stores for the value of store coupons, the store absorbs the loss. Store coupons are intended to cre-ate incentives to bring in new customers and keep regular customers loyal, so overage allowances depend on the region, the particular store, and in some cases, the manager. Accordingly, here is yet another reason why you need to know your store's policy: and how it functions under both corporate and internal management rules. Also, you should know that smart registers have the capability to adjust all applied coupons and coupon combinations to equal only that of the item price, and thus generally do not allow for overages.

Other times, overage occurs when a single coupon alone is greater than the cost of the item for which it is intended. For example, one August, Walgreens® offered the Air Wick® Compact I-Motion for $3.99, which was half off its original price. During that same week, the SmartSource® insert offered a $4.00/1 ($4.00 off one product) coupon for an Air Wick I-Motion Starter Kit. Now, Walgreens is one of those stores with smart registers, so the coupon beeped when the cashier tried to scan it. In such a case, the store had to accept the coupon, but not at its full value of $4.00, but, rather at $3.99. In similar situations, many cashiers will tell you they cannot take the coupon at all, but they will be wrong and you'll need to have your wits about you.

A single coupon's value for a single item should **never** exceed the cost of the item, or the retailer will not be properly reimbursed for the amount by the manufacturer. In such a situation, the cashier must price-modify the value of the coupon down to the item price. Retailers have this authority, though some might not know they do. It is very common to encounter a cashier who does not know how to adjust the price, and you'll need to call over a manager. A second option, though not the one I prefer because the store is being refunded by the product's manufacturer, is to adjust the price up to the amount of the coupon. Either way, you may find the manager doesn't know the policy, or is in an uncooperative mood and unwilling to help. In such a case, leave! Try again another time, but don't allow yourself to be bullied into overpaying. It is absolutely acceptable to use the coupon, especially since the manufacturer will reimburse the store if the coupon amount is adjusted. Price modification of the coupon is the reasonable solution.

The Beauty of BOGOs

Buy one get one coupons are not the same as free item coupons, but more like 50 percent off each item being purchased. Sometimes cashiers are confused if you stack a BOGO (buy one get one) coupon against a BOGO sale, but it doesn't change the intent of the coupon, which is to allow you to purchase two items at half the cost. BOGO sales are advertised in flyers, on store websites, and on signs throughout stores, so be on the lookout and start to pair them with your Qs.

In a buy one get one sale, you may use either one BOGO coupon or two single-item coupons, but you must not mix them. The process can be tricky, so let me simplify. In a buy one get one sale, you purchase two items. A BOGO coupon also covers two items, so it can be used; if you have a coupon that covers one item, you may use two of them, but if your coupon is for money off two items, like a $0.75/2 coupon, then you can only use one. No combination of the aforementioned can be used either. That's because the coupon(s) used must apply to only two items.

A good rule of thumb is to follow the denominator on the coupons. Let's look at a typical coupon pictured on the next page. It reads, "Save $1.00 of any Two V8 100% Vegetable Juice." When I write down my list and match coupons, I want to save time so I'll write $1/2 V8 Q. That means I have a coupon for $1.00 off two V8 bottles. Notice the numerator is the dollar or cent value of the coupon and

the denominator covers the amount of products I must buy. I can use this V8® coupon on a BOGO sale, because the sale itself also covers two items. With a quick look to my denominator—two—I can assure myself that I am all set.

Let's see how this works in practice. A $4/2 is a $4.00 coupon off the purchase of two items. Since a buy one get one sale covers two items, the $4/2 coupon would apply. Similarly, it would be okay to use two $2/1 coupons, as the coupon refers to $2.00 off one item. You may also use one BOGO coupon, covering two items, on a buy one get one sale.

For example, let's pretend your store is offering a buy one get one sale on Got2B™ Smooth Operator Smoothing Hairspray, which averages $6.00 at most stores. You pick up two bottles and head over to the register. You use a BOGO (buy one get one) manufacturer coupon on the items. The cashier will ring in the items first, and you'll see the original scanned price drop from $12.00 to $6.00 because of the sale. When he scans the coupon, the total will drop to zero, and both items are then free! Since you purchased two items, it is like you used the "buy one" part of the coupon against the free sale item and the "get one free" part of the coupon against the $6.00 full-priced item. You are purchasing two bottles of hairspray and your coupon covers two products, so you are using it ethically.

A BOGO NO-NO

Never use two BOGO (buy one get one) coupons on a single BOGO sale, as that would be a form of theft. (Two BOGO Qs does not equal two Items.) If you are reading about deals other people post online and see this kind of coupon use, do not follow the suggestion. Further, if you are comfortable with the store management where the deal is suggested, please give them a heads up so they can instruct cashiers to watch out. By doing so, you show that you are a couponer who is to be respected, and should you ever make a legitimate mistake, they will know it is unintentional.

Something for Free

Free item coupons are a whole other game. In the first place, manufacturers rarely give these out. They are sometimes referred to as **Full-Value coupons (FVQ)**. Manufacturers may send them to you during a new product launch, as a thank-you for contacting the company and telling them that you like the product, or as a response by customer service to a reasonable complaint. Calling, emailing, or writing letters to your favorite manufacturers, as well as being part of any reward programs like Pampers® Gift to Grow or My Coke® Rewards, are excellent ways to induce manufacturers to provide free item Qs. Also, sign up for store loyalty cards or email lists, like those offered by CVS® pharmacies, Lands' End clothing retailer, and Michaels® craft store, to name a few. You'll never know when you'll find FVQs (full-value coupons) in your email inbox or post mailbox.

Free item coupons are best used during a Buy-One-Get-One (BOGO) sale, in conjunction with a Catalina sale

(CAT—Catalina Marketing promotion that earns additional coupons for specific items bought), or for items needed as fillers (more than $2.00) to raise transaction totals.

A free item coupon can make for memorable stacking. My coupon buddy, Jenn, wrote an email to Pampers® raving about their Dry Max diapers, and Proctor & Gamble (Pampers' parent company) in return sent her a coupon for free diapers. Being the master couponer she is, Jenn didn't run out and buy some Pampers, immediately wasting her free coupon, but rather patiently waited for one of those lovely Proctor & Gamble (P&G) Catalinas to come along. Proctor & Gamble frequently offers Catalinas where you must spend $25.00 on P&G products in order to earn $10.00 on your next order (OYNO). And because Jenn knows that combining a free-item manufacturer coupon with a store coupon for overage on an item is a perfectly valid use of stacking, she maximized the value of that free-item coupon by stacking it along with others as a filler for P&G products. While generally fillers are items of value equal to or less than $2.00, purchasing an item with a full-value coupon can be considered a filler. The transaction total still goes up, but your out-of-pocket expense is zero. Not only did Jenn get the Pampers® free, but she got several other P&G products and a $10 On Your Next Order coupon as well.

Time's Up

Finally, we need to discuss what to do with expired coupons. Many stores, like CVS®, Kohl's®, and Bed, Bath & Beyond®, take expired coupons. Some stores place a limit on expired coupons based on the time that has passed between expiration to use, usually one to two weeks. Others take only expired store coupons and not expired manufacturer coupons. Acceptance of expired coupons varies widely, even within franchises of the same chain. This is another example of why you have to know your store, because the corporate and store policies on expired coupons may differ. I know stores within walking distance of each other where different expired-coupon policies are applied.

Also, please consider sending expired coupons you are unable to use to our overseas military. Expired coupons sent overseas will be distributed to our soldiers, where the coupons are accepted in their commissaries. Coupons should be sorted into food and non-food groups before sending.

ONE SHALL STAND, ONE SHALL FALL

Sisters Heather and Janet were competitive about couponing and shopped at most of the same stores. Having both taken my class, they set out each week to beat each other in overall savings. Before Halloween, their favorite store's price-scan machines printed out one-day coupons good for $5.00 off Halloween decorations or costumes. Two days after Halloween, when all holiday products had dropped in price by 50%, both Heather and Janet separately went to the store. Janet picked up a black cat decoration marked down from $10.00 to $4.99, used her $5.00 SQ (store coupon), meaning it was free, and returned home to pack it away for next year.

Heather, unfortunately, didn't get to the store until after the staff had changed over. When Heather brought jack-o-lantern lights and a pumpkin tablecloth to the counter, the cashier refused the coupon, saying it was expired. Heather tried to argue that this store accepted coupons up to two weeks after the expiration date, but the cashier responded that the policy did not extend to clearance items. Heather left without her jack-o-lantern lights and tablecloth, disappointed that only hours earlier her sister had scored on the black cat.

Your Mileage May Vary

You may also notice these letters written on coupon blog sites—YMMV (**Your Mileage May Vary**)—around a given scenario. Your Mileage May Vary is used to describe the different store-to-store policies with regard to overages, doubling, expired coupon use, personal results, buy one get one sales, and free item coupons. Your Mileage May Vary can even apply to item prices. Sometimes, for example, a coupon's value is higher than the price of an item.

While a friend may be able to use her overage toward another product, you might be denied use of the coupon altogether. The earlier example of the sisters Heather and Janet, with their different outcomes using their expired Qs, is also called YMMV. Sometimes, too, you will see a price given on an Internet site, but your regional store may price the item differently. All of these are examples of why your mileage may vary (YMMV).

Putting It All Together

Now it's time to really make the run, by buying a lot of additional products to make the overall price lower. To build this scenario, we will use a combination of store and manufacturer's coupons, a BOGO sale and corresponding BOGO coupons, coupon adjustment because of overage, and the earning of ECBs (ExtraCare Bucks). Also, notice that this scenario includes the use of fillers to raise our transaction total over $20.00 and thus allowing us to use a $5/$20 Trans Q (transaction coupon). In this case, the fillers are SoBe® drinks.

Transaction:
$2.99 Colgate® Total® Toothpaste
$7.00 Crest® Pro Health (2)
$1.98 CVS® Tissues (2)

$1.98 Cat Litter (2)
$5.60 SoBe® Drinks (4)
$2.99 Aussie® product
=$22.54 subtotal
–$$5/$20 CVS® TQ (transaction coupon)
–$5.60 (2) SoBe BOGO MQs
–$2.00 (2) Crest® $1/1 MQs
–$1.00 Colgate® MQ
–$1.00 Aussie MQ
–$1/2 CVS tissues SQ
–$6.90 ECBs (adjusted down from $6.94 due to over-
   age—YMMV)
–$0.04 OOP (Out of Pocket)
–$11.00 ECBs earned ($2 Aussie, $2 Colgate,
   $7 Crest)
= +$10.96 MM (Money Maker)

Now, that's a deal! How did we pull this off? First, remember your five basic steps to build a scenario: (1) Pick a store, (2) Make a list, (3) Note the specials, (4) Check the coupon databases, and (5) STACK, STACK, STACK! Every item on the list was chosen because a coupon could be used for it. The store was chosen to gain the extra savings because of the store's rewards program, which translates to savings.

You can make your scenario as small or grand as you like. I tend to make constrained scenarios with as few products as possible. However, I always try to maximize as many deal-saving techniques as I can for those products, such as mixing many types of coupons together. I also try to take advantage of buy one get one sales and overage when-ever I can. So, start small, but plan big. You have the tools now to build your own.

READY TO GRAB THAT TOOL BELT?

1. **What is the first step to great scenario-building?**
   a. Make a list.
   b. Pick a store.
   c. Relax.

2. **What is the second step to great scenario-building?**
   a. Make a list.
   b. Note the specials.
   c. Pick a store.

3. **If your store doubles Q values up to $1.98, which coupon is worth more: $0.75 or $1.00?**
   a. $1.00
   b. They are the same.
   c. $0.75

4. **What are Coupon Doublers?**
   a. Special coupons used with regular coupons to double them.
   b. Special sales when coupons are doubled.
   c. A bowling term.

5. **What is the third step to great scenario-building?**
   a. Check the coupon databases.
   b. Stick to your list and shop off hours.
   c. Note the specials.

6. **What best describes Overage?**
   a. Using coupons to make an item free.
   b. Using coupons to make money on an item.
   c. Using coupons to make an item half-off.

7. Which Q can be combined with a BOGO sale?

  a. A BOGO coupon.

  b. A $1/2 coupon.

  c. Either.

8. What are some the variables mentioned with YMMV?

  a. Product price.

  b. Acceptance of overage.

  c. Both

9. What don't I recommend doing with your expired coupons?

  a. Throw them out.

  b. See if you can use still them.

  c. Send them to our overseas military for use in their commissaries.

10. What is the fifth and final step to great scenario-building?

  a. Note the specials.

  b. Read the chapter again.

  c. STACK, STACK, STACK!

Answers: 1. b, 2. a, 3. c, 4. a, 5. c, 6. b, 7. c, 8. c, 9. a, 10. c

CHAPTER 5

Understanding Catalinas

(The CATs Are Here!)

A S WE HAVE SEEN, COUPONS ARE ONE OF MANY marketing techniques to persuade you to buy a particular product. Coupons can be offered to the general public, such as the ones you find within your Sunday newspaper inserts. Manufacturers also market directly to particular buyers, sending out coupons specific to your buying habits. This approach makes a lot of sense. When the coupons you receive are connected to your buying habits, you are more likely to use them. Marketing based on buyer habits is used especially at the point of sale, or when you are in the store shopping. Really, it is just another way for manufacturers to get you to buy their products, but this time they are targeting products you are more inclined to buy.

For instance, point-of-sale coupons encourage shop-

pers to buy a larger product size than normal. They can also encourage you to buy a product that goes along with something you are planning to buy. If manufacturers place this taggie for Hershey's® Pieces on the soda bottle you were already purchasing, maybe you'll grab a Hershey's Pieces Pouch instead of the bag of Lay's® potato chips you were planning on getting to go along with the soda. The manufacturer knows that most people grabbing a 20 oz soda usually buy a snack to go along with it, so they hope to persuade you to buy one of their products.

Other point-of-sale techniques include use of sample tables, unadvertised sales, manager specials, point-of-purchase displays, rebates, and impulse items at the registers. The most important technique for the savvy couponer to utilize is the Catalina promotion. With these shopper-driven promotions, you earn special coupons that are printed out at the cash register and can be used on your next purchase.

There is simply nothing better than shopping with Catalinas (CATs). With them you can pay not only for the product they are promoting but also other non-coupon products. CATs often print out of the checkout printer machines on top or next to grocery store registers. You know all those coupons cashiers hand you wrapped up with your receipt? They are CAT Qs. They are also my not-so-secret true love. It is through using CATs that the super savings begin. Still don't know what a CAT is? You will. Don't live near a CAT store? Move!

Catalina coupons—called CATs, Catalinas, or CAT Qs— get their name because they are distributed by Catalina Marketing, a company that specializes in consumer-driven sales. Catalina Marketing controls a massive database of consumer information based on over a year's worth of shopping trends that stores and manufacturers can use to create shopper-tailored promotions.

GOT A CAT STORE?

To find a few CAT stores in your area, check this quick list:

East Coast: ACME®, A&P, Food Lion, Hannaford®, Stop & Shop®, and Weis

Midwest: Albertsons®, Giant Eagle®, King Soopers®, and Kroger®

North: Giant®, Hy-Vee®, Kmart®, Meijer®, Smith's®, and Walgreens®

South; Dillons®, H.E.B.®, fry's®, Pathmark®, Schnucks®, Sweetbay™, and Winn Dixie®

West Coast: Fred Meyer®, fry's®, Jewel-osco®, Ralphs®, Safeway®, Save Mart®, and QFC

There are different types of CAT Qs. Sometimes CAT Qs are just cents or dollars off items, like regular coupons, but are dispensed from the CAT machine, like this $1.00 CAT Q for Ocean Spray®. You may get the coupons because of your lifestyle shopping, which means the coupon is driven because of the things you normally buy. Other times, the coupon you get is triggered by the UPC of a particular

product scanned. For example, if you buy a box of Kellogg's Frosted Mini-Wheats Blueberry Muffin cereal, you might receive a CAT Q that offers $0.75 off your next purchase of Kellogg's® Frosted Mini-Wheats® Strawberry Delight, because they want you try their other flavored Mini-Wheats cereal.

Other times CATs are transaction coupons good at the store where they were generated, encouraging you to get your purchase totals up, like here with this $3.00 off $35.00 or more Stop & Shop® CAT Q. CATs can also be On Your Next Order (or shopping trip) coupons earned from

meeting its purchase requirements, like here with these two pictured $5.00 OYNO coupons that were triggered through purchasing select General Mills, P&G, and/or Kraft® products.

They look different but work the same. They can be used against any product(s) purchased at the store, except tobacco and alcohol.

CAT promotions require the purchaser to buy certain products in order to earn a coupon for use on a future transaction, like "Buy $20 of Gillette® products, get $5 on your next purchase." The ONYO coupon, triggered by meeting the CAT purchase requirements, is the type of CAT that the true couponer wants in his or her hand.

For example, during a March Frozen Food Month, several different types of CATs were triggered by purchasing a combination of select frozen food products. You had to buy those products during a single transaction to generate the OYNO coupon. The coupons are usually good for two weeks, but because I am lazy and will forget to use them, I often make a second transaction while I am at the store to benefit from the coupon. Suppose I am at the grocery store and know I am going to earn $10 OYNO coupon from a CAT promotion, because I saw a printed promotion on the register tape or checked a couponing blog ahead of time and plan to buy the products required to trigger it. I will pull aside $10 worth of produce to buy after my first transaction, thus paying for my fresh, coupon-free veggies with the new coupon and heading home without more papers to file and track. Another option, which may prove easier for you, is simply to wrap your loyalty card with the earned $10 CAT money and put it in your wallet. You can use it next time you shop.

CAT COVERED?

According to Catalina Marketing, their Catalina promotions are utilized in more than 24,000 grocery and supercenters and another 18,000 pharmacies across the nation.

Along with CAT coupons, the checkout printer machines sometimes dispense CAT information, telling about upcoming Catalina promotions like this typical one pictured.

The information informs us of the promotion dates, 10/4–10/31, what we need to buy, and how much CAT money we'll earn. Most CAT promotions are set up like this: buying a smaller amount of items yields a lower-value coupon, and buying more items yields a higher-value

coupon. Nature Valley® details the terms of the promotion in black on the right where it says, "Buy (2) Get $1.50, Buy (3) Get $2.50, Buy (5) or more get $3.50 coupon off your next order." Because we know the lingo, we couponers note the CAT like this: B2G$1.50, B3G$2.50, B5+G$3.50 OYNO.

Other CAT promotions are based on dollar amount, rather than product quantity, but the information on the cash register tape still tells us what we need to buy. The coupon to the left tells us that $25 (pre-sale/pre-coupon dollars) of participating ConAgra Foods®, Georgia Pacific, Dannon®, and Dr. Pepper® Snapple® Group must be bought between 03/05 and 03/11. (ConAgra® is the parent company of products like Chef Boyardee®, Healthy Choice®, Egg Beaters®, Hunt's®, and Alexia®; Georgia Pacific is the maker of Brawny®, Sparkle®, Mardi Gras®, Angel Soft®, Quilted Northern®, and Dixie®.) The promotional information also tells us what kind of OYNO coupon we'd get if we meet the requirements. Here, it is two $5.00 coupons.

You can buy the triggering items, fail to pair them with any coupons, and you'd still get back $10.00. However, if you're really smart, you'll pick those items for which you have matching coupons—and that are also on sale. Let's say you could buy $25.00 worth of pre-sale items on sale for $19.00. You also use $7.00 worth of coupons for RO*TEL® diced tomatoes (ConAgra brand), plus Mott's® apple juice, and Nantucket Nectars® (both Dr. Pepper Snapple brands). That would bring your out-of-pocket costs down to $12.00. That's $12.00 before you receive the $10.00 in CAT Qs, good for anything you purchase next time at the store! You bought $25.00 worth of items for $2.00! Now do you see why I love Catalinas?

When CAT Qs are not general dollar-off OYNOs, the coupons can be restrictively for your purchase of select items like meat, seafood, poultry, or health-care items, as shown here.

Other times, OYNOs are for things like free milk—usually

the result of buying five gallons and the sixth is free. If you buy cereal, there may be a CAT promotion for savings towards your banana purchase, which are my particular favorite because I buy bananas every week.

In stores like Target®, the earned coupon will be a store gift card rather than an OYNO Q. (This is different than a gift card CAT earned by buying gift cards, as we usually see every December, where you also get a gift card as the reward.) Instead, Target® will give you a $5.00 gift card for buying 10 of one type of product or maybe $25.00 worth of a manufacturer's brand. While the gift card-earning CAT isn't necessarily a traditional CAT offered through Catalina Marketing, we still refer to the promotion as a CAT because you must purchase set products to activate the reward you can later use. The earned gift card acts exactly like an OYNO coupon—you can use it for your next purchase—yet, it is easier to fit in your wallet and less likely to get lost. I am still waiting for CAT coupons that can be loaded directly on your loyalty card. Think that's next? I hope so!

While the CAT printer machines are the best source for finding out what CATs are being offered, you can also check the couponing blogs, store flyers, or do a Google search. Good blog sites keep track of many of the Catalina promotions for you. Although I would prefer an easy-to-navigate list, most of these sites include the CAT promotions in the weekly section of the grocery store tabs.

How does that work? Let's say you live in Pennsylvania and you want to know what CATs Giant Eagle® grocery is offering this week. You can go to A Thrifty Mom (www.athriftymom.com) to check her list. Simply go to the grocery tab and click on the Giant Eagle button. Then you'll be linked to the week's deals and any current CATs, along with matching coupons. The information will be listed among other sale information like this:

$3 OYNO WYB 6 Pillsbury® Products Below:
Golden Layers®, Grands! Biscuits, Cinnamon Rolls, or Crescent Rolls $1 each
$.30/2 or $.40/3 Pillsbury Refrigerated Grands! Biscuits, any—11–21 SS
$1/3 or $.30/2 Pillsbury Refrigerated Grands or Grands! Jr. biscuits—11–14 GM
$.30/2 printable (This would be a link you'd click to get the printable coupon)

Final Price = $.20 each for Biscuits after Catalina!

A Thrifty Mom also covers weekly sales for the following grocery stores: Albertsons®, Fred Meyer®, Kroger, Safeway®, Food Lion, Giant, Eagle®, Ralphs®, Giant, Vons®, Winn Dixie, and Shaw's® among others, all with weekly sales and corresponding CAT info.

Another method is to do a general internet search. Just type the name of the store you want to search followed by either Catalinas or Catalina Deals, and the search will produce current links to those sites that keep track of CATs. For example, typing "Shaws Catalinas" generates wonderful links by www.afullcup.com and www.mavinofsavin.com, both with up-to-date CAT information for Shaw's®.

Other times, you can access CAT information by signing up for a store's or a manufacturer's email list. This email sent to RedPlum™ email-subscribers contains information about a CAT deal for two OYNO coupons—$1.00 off Orville Redenbacher's Poppycock and $1.50 off soda—with the purchase of two Orville Reden-bacher's® 3-pack or larger popcorn. So if your grocery store prints CAT Qs, you would want  to consider whether you can match the purchase with coupons to buy the initial two 3-packs.

Let's say you do the minimum on this CAT because you don't need thirty boxes of microwave popcorn in the house. How does it turn out? You can get a three-count box of Orville Redenbacher's® Butter popcorn for $1.89, so you buy two ($3.78). There are usually $0.40/1 3ct+ Orville Redenbacher microwave popcorn coupons in Smart-Source® inserts, so you'd want to clip two. $3.78–(2) $0.40 Qs–$0.80 Q doubling amount = $2.18 out of pocket (OOP). Each box of popcorn has two free DVD rentals in them and the purchase of the two boxes yields a $1.00 popcorn OYNO and $1.50 soda OYNO. Now, because you are doing this the simplest way, you leave the $1.00 popcorn OYNO on top of the register for someone else and grab a two-liter of soda for $1.50, using the OYNO and making it free. Your total result is this: $2.18 OOP for six bags of microwave popcorn, a two-liter of soda and four DVD rentals. Not bad for almost $10 worth of items!

Sometimes CAT information is listed in flyers. Look at this advertised P&G CAT that was advertised right on the back page of the weekly flyer.

The fine print notes the dates and tells you that it is a CAT with a threshold of $25.00 in order to get the $5.00 OYNO. Remember, the $25.00 is the pre-sale, pre-coupon price at grocery stores, so get the cheaper items that match up best with coupons. If your store accepts both manufacturer and store coupons, you can double up. On top of all of those savings, you then earn a $5.00 CAT.

With all these sources for getting and keeping track of CAT info, things can get a bit confusing. I suggest keeping a Word or Pages document somewhere on your desktop and updating it with each piece of new CAT info you find. I keep a running document where I add new CAT info to the top as I acquire it and delete expired CAT info whenever they end. This way, my list tends to be comprehensive, current, and easily sortable. I encourage you to use this technique for yourself or find another method that works for you.

STICKY FINGERS?

If you ever use self-checkout and see CAT information or CAT Qs sitting on top of the printer machine, grab them! They are not specific to your loyalty card, and any left there are free for your grabbing.

Finally, when discussing CATs, we should talk about troubleshooting, because sometimes you will buy all the specified items for a CAT promotion and you won't get your OYNO coupon. CATs sometimes fail to print because of faulty checkout printer machines, empty ink cartridges or mistakes in how the products are rung up at the register. Other times, your CAT might get crumpled in the machine, print illegibly with smeared ink, or not print at all. If this happens, the problem can be resolved in several ways.

If you are in a grocery store, do not call over a supervisor or bother the customer service desk. Most grocery employees have no idea what CATs even are, or how to remedy the issue. In the case of grocery store CAT problems, go back home and contact Catalina Marketing. You can email them at coupon@catalinamarketing.com or call 1-888-8coupon and choose option 3. You will need to tell them where you were shopping, the time and date of purchase, what your loyalty card number is if you used a loyalty card, and what CAT you didn't receive. Assuming your purchases met the specifications set by the promotion, the company will then mail you a coupon with an adjusted expiration date for using the OYNO.

Should you be shopping in a store whose CAT Qs are printed on cash register tape (CRT) as part of the store rewards program, like CVS® with ECBs (ExtraCare Bucks), your first step is to make the cashier aware of the mistake. They can scan the receipt and enter in the ECB code to generate the reward. CRT CAT coupons work this way because the reward is being offered by the store. In the event that the cashier is unable to do so, resort to asking for a manager's help. If the coupons are printed from the cash registers instead of a coupon printer machine, it is technically not a CAT but a CRT, so do not contact Catalina Marketing.

CAT VS. CRT

CRT—anything printed on the same paper as your receipt, usually attached to it and generated from the cash register itself.

CAT—technically anything that prints from that little printer machine next to or above the cash register. The cashier usually hands the pieces to you along with the receipt.

Overlap—CATs can be a type of CRT in stores like with Walgreens Register Rewards, where the term CAT refers to the promotion deal triggered by buying certain items. CAT is also used colloquially to refer to CRT money, like ECBs or UPs.

CAT GOT YOUR TONGUE?

1. On what kind of marketing are Catalinas based?
   a. Consumer-driven.
   b. Mass mailing.
   c. Internet advertising.

2. Point-of-sale techniques do not include which of the following pair?
   a. Sample tables and point-of-purchase displays.
   b. Unadvertised sales and random mailings.
   c. Rebates and Catalinas.

3. CATs get their nickname from which company?
   a. Catalina Marketers.
   b. Catalina Marketing Promotions.
   c. Catalina Marketing.

4. Where can you not find printed CAT Qs?
   a. On CRTs.
   b. From a checkout printer machine.
   c. In a flyer or insert.

5. Which best describes a CAT?
   a. An OYNO coupon generated from purchasing a specific set of products.
   b. An item coupon good for two weeks.
   c. Triple barcodes and store logos.

6. Traditional Catalinas are triggered by …
   a. Pre-coupon price.
   b. Pre-sale price.
   c. Pre-sale and pre-coupon prices.

7. **What is the most reliable way to find current CAT information?**
   a. From the checkout printer machine.
   b. On couponing blogs.
   c. Doing a Google™ search.

8. **What is the suggested way to organize current CAT info?**
   a. Keep your flyers handy.
   b. Just check the couponing blogs.
   c. Use a Word or Pages document.

9. **What is not a reason the CAT doesn't print?**
   a. Ink issues.
   b. A massive hurricane hit your store.
   c. It gets crumpled in the checkout printer machine.

10. **Which of the following is not a good way to resolve a CAT printing problem at grocery stores?**
   a. Go to Customer Service.
   b. Call 1-888-8coupon, option 3.
   c. Email coupon@catalinamarketing.com.

Answers: 1. a, 2. b, 3. c, 4. c, 5. a, 6. c, 7. a, 8. c, 9. b, 10. a

CHAPTER 6:

Shopping for Groceries

WHEN *NBC NIGHTLY NEWS* ASKED TO INTER-view me, I was admittedly excited, but also a lit-tle nervous. I wasn't afraid of looking silly or not being able to produce a good savings, but worried that people would see the segment and assume I spent hours each week prepping to shop. By now you know, I do not. I actually spend minutes to prep and minutes to shop. I was also concerned about people's perceptions that in order to save I must buy terrible pre-packaged food. I had actu-ally been panned in comments stemming from previous *Boston Globe* articles where several people referred to me as a "Cheetos Eater." FYI—I hate Cheetos®, but I do love to eat. So aside from the candy I added at the register to get my total over zero, here it is—the actual food I purchased for the *NBC Nightly News,* for which I paid only $0.42 for $167.00 of food!

Broccoli crowns
2lb baby carrots
1 head Boston lettuce
Shallots
Sweet potatoes
1lb strawberries
12 oz Cedar's® spinach dip
(2) 8 oz Cedar's Lemon hummus
8 oz Cedar's Vegetable hummus
8 pk Honest Kids® Organic Straw/Lemonade
Naked® Juice Green Machine
(2) Naked Juice 100% Blue Machine
20 oz Dasani Water
20 oz Aquafina®
2 dozen Eggland's Best® Natural eggs
2 gallons Garelick Farms® Natural skim milk
3 Chobani® Greek yogurt
(4) Robert's Pirate's Booty
Newman's® Organic Herb spaghetti sauce
14.5 oz College Inn® low-sodium broth
12 pk Sargento® Colby Jack cheese sticks
(2) 64 oz Tropicana® Pure Premium®
    Low Acid orange juice
Slow-cooked chicken soup
(3) Lay's® chips
1lb unsalted butter
(2) M&M's®
Lifesavers® Gummies pouch
(2) 12 pk Coke Zero®
(2) 20 oz Coke Zero
12 pk Diet Sprite®
Nature's Promise® 100% whole wheat bread
Arnold® Whole Grain 100% whole wheat bread
(2) Arnold Sandwich Thins
Nature's Promise organic multigrain bread
Immaculate Baking Co. organic cookie dough

Green Giant® Steam baby sweet peas
Green Giant Brussels sprouts in butter
20 oz SoBe® Lifewater
Perdue® drumsticks
Perdue chicken nuggets
1lb Shady Brook Farms® lean ground turkey breast
(2) Hillshire Farms® turkey kielbasas
(2) Cedar's® wraps—spinach
(2) Cedar's pita chips

After absorbing the last five chapters, you may think you are all set, but believe me, we still have a long way to go. Now you need to apply what you've learned about coupons to the actual grocery store where you shop. I suggest using the tools set out in this chapter to master one single grocer of your choice; later, you can use the techniques you mastered at other stores where savings may be even greater. If you generally shop at the store with lowest everyday prices, begin there. While the cheapest store for the non-couponer is unlikely to be the cheapest for a super-couponer, it is a fine place to start. Once you achieve mastery, move on.

This chapter will show you what to look for and how to apply your trained eye. First, you must know the store's coupon policy and how to get a copy for yourself. Second, you need to look through flyers to know what specialty sales the store is offering. Then, you'll want to combine coupons and the special sales strategies we have discussed in the last few chapters, like Doublers, One-Day Sales, Weekly Meal Deals, Pick 4s, CATs, and others. Finally, you'll follow the *Lazy Couponer's* process for shopping, including list-writing and navigating specific stores.

Don't Sweat the Sale Cycles

You absolutely do not need to follow complicated rules, like tracking sales over months and then stockpiling like crazy. That is a standard technique in the couponing world: chase sales, which generally run on a four-to-six-week cycle; save matching coupons to use then; and buy lots of that product to create a stockpile. Don't buy in to all that. The overall concept is a decent idea, but who has all that time? I don't. I have a student who bought a cow—I don't know how—and now it is in her freezer! While that is certainly an option, I suggest you shop smarter so you won't need to exert that much energy or take up so much space.

It is a good idea to keep the sale cycles in the back of your mind, because if you haven't seen a sale for a certain product in a while, its cycle is likely coming back around and you may want to wait. But other than that, don't worry about it. Continue to buy the food items you buy each week. Don't stock up on 15 bottles of ketchup because it is on sale; you'll never go through all those bottles before another sale comes around. On the other hand, if you are running low on ketchup and you haven't seen a ketchup sale this month, maybe you could wait until next week to get it. The system really is that simple. Do your best to catch the sales and match your coupons, but don't bog yourself down with the chase.

Saving money at the grocery store merely translates to shopping with forethought. Some techniques should be common sense, like buying produce seasonally. Why spend $5.00 for four ounces of blueberries when, in season, they are half the price? Grab an apple instead. Do you still want the blueberries? Explore alternatives to see if they work for you first. (And no, you don't have to buy 15 pints during the summer and freeze them all.) Here is one option to consider. Cascadian Farm® sells delicious organic blueberries in the frozen aisle for half the price of the fresh off-season ones, and choosing a bag of frozen berries when the craving hits is much easier than stuffing your freezer full of them in the middle of the summer. But before you buy, check the databases, because I am sure you can find a coupon for them, too. Frozen blueberries not your thing? Bolthouse® and Odwalla® both make awesome blueberry juices, and guess what: you can find coupons for each of them, too. Still not convinced? Then buy yourself that overpriced fresh produce and enjoy every bite—just try to pay for it with a CAT Q.

While I don't suggest chasing sales, I will tell you a bit about how grocery stores run their sale cycles. One thought to keep in mind is that during certain months, nationally sponsored food items are at their cheapest. Nationally sponsored food months are as follows: January—oatmeal, February—canned food and hot breakfast, March—frozen food, June—dairy, July—ice cream, October–seafood. Why do you need to know this? You don't, but finding matching Catalinas (CATs) or coupons is easier if you have a general idea about upcoming sales. For example, last July, Edy's® offered a Catalina promotion where you earned an On Your Next Order (OYNO) coupon if you purchased a set amount of Edy's ice cream. (The coupon value varied according the amount of Edy's you purchased.) At the same time, stores were selling Edy's in a buy one get one (BOGO) sale. By combining the BOGO sale and the CAT, it was cheaper to purchase four gallons of Edy's instead of two, because purchasing the third gallon generated an ONYO coupon that offset the price of the ice cream, as well as earned a fourth (and free) gallon. By knowing that July is National Ice Cream month, you'll be more likely to look for the matching CAT when July comes around. I will admit that I almost stumble on it each year because my son's birthday is at the end of the month and I tend to look for ice cream then anyhow. However, if keeping track of sales months is too much for you to think about, don't sweat it. A two-for-one deal is still a great value you'd catch just by going to the grocery store.

A second important food related sale cycle revolves around the year's major holidays and events. They are as follows: January has the Super Bowl; February has Valentine's Day and Chinese New Year; April has Easter; May has Memorial Day and Cinco de Mayo; June/July have the Fourth of July; August/September have Back to School (Labor Day); October has Halloween; November has Thanksgiving and Holiday Baking; December has Hanukkah, Christmas, and Kwanzaa. Most people already know turkeys go on sale about two weeks before Thanksgiving and candy is best purchased during October and February. But take a step beyond that. Start to think about the after-holiday clearance sales, too. Be on the lookout a week after the holiday when overstock items go on clearance.

Know How to Shop, Not Where to Shop

The current wave of couponers also insists you pick the right store, while I say that's hogwash! Once you learn the ins and outs, you can make any store work for you. You simply need to know the store and its policies, and then apply your *Lazy Couponer* techniques.

Let's begin with a few basic questions. Does your favorite grocery store accept manufacturers' coupons? If so, do they also offer store coupons? What about their policies on doublers, free-item, and BOGO Qs? Do they set limits on how many coupons you can hand the cashier during a transaction? Does the store regularly double or triple coupons, and with what limitations? Does the store feature CAT coupons or CAT promotions? Can you load coupons directly onto your loyalty card?

Once you know the answers to questions like these, you will know how to shop at the store. With coupon use on the rise throughout the country, many stores have begun to post their coupon policies right on their websites. For your convenience, I've included a list of links for the most popular nationwide stores at the end of this chapter. However, if you don't see your favorite store on the list, simply email or write to ask about their coupon policy. For mail, I would contact corporate customer service. When using email you'll usually find a "contact us" link on the store's website. Note: if you plan to use the policy before you have the opportunity to establish relationships with cashiers and store managers, think about requesting the policy by mail, because it looks more official than a printed email. If you shop at a store with difficult cashiers and/or managers, definitely request an official policy by mail.

Once you receive the coupon policy and read it through, you are ready to use the newspaper flyers to their maximum effect. To properly read store flyers, you need a critical eye, as you need to know the store's habits. Every store offers different specialty sales for the week and in order to capitalize on them, you have to first know what types of sales they have.

POLICY HUNTER

To Whom It May Concern:
I am interested in learning about the coupon policy for (store name)_____. Could you please forward it to me via email (or mail) and address any of the questions listed below if not explicitly outlined in the policy?
Thank you,

_____.

1. Do you offer store coupons? Where are they found?
2. Do you accept Internet printed coupons? Can they be printed in black and white?
3. Do you accept BOGO coupons? Can they be used with a BOGO sale?
4. Do you accept free-item or full-value coupons?
5. Are there maximum coupon value limitations?
6. What is the overage policy?
7. Do you regularly double or triple coupons? Do you ever have special promotion times when doubling or tripling occurs or when coupon doublers are offered? Where can they be found?
8. Can e-coupons be loaded directly on to my loyalty card? If I also present a physical coupon at the time of purchase, which one is applied to my transaction?
9. Do you accept competitors' coupons or match prices?
10. Do you limit the number of coupons I can use per transaction?
11. Are variances from the corporate policy at the discretion of store management? What about anything not explicitly written within the policy?

For example, many store flyers include coupons (Qs) embedded in them called in-ad Qs. Some store flyers only include store Qs, some only manufacturer Qs, while others embed both types. Other stores use flyers to distribute in-ad coupons during special promotion weeks.

If your grocer doesn't embrace the use of any in-ad coupons, then you won't want to waste any time looking for them. If the flyer is likely to include in-ad coupons then you'll want to look them over more carefully, so that's why you need to know how your store's coupons work.

Other types of values to look for in grocery store flyers are one- to three-day sales, which most stores utilize. During a one- to three-day sale, you will find special prices for a limited time, after which items return to their regular prices, even within the same week. So, if your grocer begins its flyer on Thursday and you shop on Sunday, you will miss all the 3-day sale prices.

Stores also commonly promote sales based on quantity: Ten for Ten (10/$10), Twenty for Five (20/$5) and Five for Ten (5/$10). These sales are best combined with coupons that make the items free (like when paired with Chicken of the Sea® $1.00 Qs), money makers (as with doubled $0.60/1 Prince Qs) or really affordable (like when paired with $0.30/1 Francesco Rinaldi® Qs).

Another specialty sale you should look for are Weekly

Meal Deals. The basic idea is to provide an accompanying item, such as a vegetable, other side, or dessert as an inducement to buy the item they are featuring. For example, you may get a free bagged-salad if you buy a rotisserie chicken. That's where the smart couponer can make some real savings. Let's say you have a coupon to use against the bagged salad. If so, you will get money off toward the chicken—because the salad is already being offered for free.

Other specialty sales may combine a choice of several items for a set price. For example, Pick 4 Deals, when you can pick four items (usually meat) for a collective discount, are especially good for combining coupons. Here I'd choose the brand item meats, like Hormel® Pork or Cooked Perfect Meatballs, with which I can also use coupons, rather than the store-brand meats. Also look for

meats included in the sale that are marked with $1.00 or $2.00 off meat Peelies. If the package is close to its expiration date, meat department managers sometimes add discount Peelies to the packages, which can be combined with the in-ad coupon like the Pick 4.

Also, in any deal that has a set price for several items, check your receipt to see how the store processes the savings. For example, this store actually takes $5.17 off meat when you use the Pick 4 coupon, because most of the items included ring up at the sale price of $6.29. However, on occasion you may find cheaper items included in the sale, such as chicken thighs for $3.00. If that is the case, you can get four of them at a combined total of $12.00, use the coupon, and pay only $6.83 for four packages of poultry!

All in all, you need to figure out what specialty sales are offered at your grocery store. Once you do, you'll be able to locate them quickly in a flyer. Maybe your store offers a Pick 3 instead of a Pick 4, or a Deal of the Day instead of a Weekly Meal Deal. Find out. The additional savings you gain when you pair specialty sales with manufacturer coupons can bring your savings up over 30%.

The best way to manage your grocery shopping is to combine coupons, special sales like those previously mentioned, and CATs (Catalina promotions). For example, suppose it is January, National Oatmeal Month, so you know oatmeal is likely to be on sale. You keep your eyes peeled for some $0.60/1 Quaker® coupons and plan to use them along with a sale. However, when you read your store's flyer, you notice there is also a $2 OYNO CAT triggered by purchasing three or more Quick, Instant, or Old-Fashioned Oats, Oatmeal Squares, or Oatmeal to Go. Not only can you pick up the oatmeal you originally wanted to buy, but you can add two more for likely no additional cost, possibly with an overage to use toward other items. In this case, you buy three boxes of Instant Oats at $1.50 each, minus $3.60 for the three Quaker coupons that each doubled, bringing your out of pocket (OOP) expense to a whopping $0.90 and earning a $2 OYNO, which actually makes you $1.10 on the oatmeal purchase.

Sometimes it is less expensive to actually buy more

items, as demonstrated earlier. The overall cost for one box, with coupon, would have been $0.30; the price for two boxes $0.60, but buying the third box earned you money. Don't be tempted to go crazy creating a stockpile of oatmeal, not that three boxes is crazy. It can be difficult to know where to draw the line, because the extra savings can always be used for something else you are buying. Many couponers would buy 15 boxes of oatmeal on sale and that's way too much. If they are items you can use, then buy them; if not, donate them or choose to ignore the sale altogether, but always remember another sale-CAT-coupon combination will come along in a month or two.

The best grocery stores to shop offer CAT promotions, but they are even better when they have loadable loyalty cards, too. A store that offers both is really the supermarket jackpot because that means a lot less work for you. Using your loyalty card to capture e-coupons can make grocery store shopping extremely convenient. E-coupons ready to load on store loyalty cards are accepted at a wide variety of stores. Go to cellfire.com or shortcuts.com to pick your store and enter your loyalty card number. After that, just click on the E-coupon and you are ready to shop. Coupons downloaded to the loyalty card will stored in order, by expiration date, and will drop off when the coupon is used or expired.

If your store accepts e-coupons loaded directly to its loyalty cards, check what's available weekly and load them on. Still, before leaving to shop, remember to check the coupon databases for physical coupons, or other e-coupons you may have missed, to take advantage of those with the highest values.

E-COUPON CARDS ACCEPTED HERE

Baker's, Carrs, City Market®, Dillons, Food4Less®, Fred Meyer®, Fry's®, Genuardi's®, Giant Eagle®, Gerbes®, Hilander, JayC, King Soopers®, Kroger, Owens®, Pavilions®, Pay Less, QFC, Ralphs®, Randalls, Safeway, Scotts, Shop 'n Save, Shop Rite®, Smith's®, Tom Thumb, and Vons®.

Grocery stores, in my mind, fall into three basic categories. Some stores do all they can to encourage ethical couponers to shop there; some accept coupons but don't go out of their way to market to couponers; and some discourage coupon use. Most stores fall into the first two types, and their eagerness to provide value makes the process of couponing relatively easy. Avoid shopping at the kinds of stores that don't accommodate couponing unless absolutely necessary. Since even small-town grocers seem to accept coupons, there is little reason to grocery-shop where coupons aren't accepted or where cashiers greet you with hostility every time you try to use several. For example, there is a large grocery store near me that is part of a big chain of retailers, and using coupons are frowned upon. Though the prices are lower and the corporate policy is to accept coupons, shopping there is unpleasant and not worth the hassle, so I shop instead at a more expensive store where they allow me to use all the coupons I want, doubling when I can and taking advantage of Catalinas. Further, the employees are supportive of my coupon use and that translates to a better experience for me. Let's explore some of the coupon policies for major grocery store chains in your area.

Safeway

The first grocery group to explore is the Safeway, Inc., group, which includes the following stores: Carrs, Dominick's, Genuardi's®, Pavilions®, Randalls,

Safeway, Tom Thumb, and Vons®. The coupon policy for U.S. Safeway stores is posted on the Safeway website at http://www.safeway.com (go to the bottom of the home page and click on "coupon policy") and is the overriding policy for all stores in the Safeway group. Safeway uses CAT promotions and allows for downloadable e-coupons to its "Club Card."

Here are the most important points about the Safeway Group coupon policy:

1. Safeway accepts store and manufacturer coupons. (Yeah!)
2. Overage is not allowed, and any coupon higher in value than the cost of the item will be adjusted down.
3. Free-item coupons are accepted, but not free Internet printables. (This rule is relatively standard among all stores now.)
4. They do not accept CAT coupons from other stores but will accept manufacturer coupons for matching manufacturer items that have logos from other stores printed on them, like a manufacturer coupon with a Target® logo on it.

5. Store personnel reserve the right to refuse coupons at their discretion. (Remember the importance of building relationships and knowing staff.)
6. Reward thresholds are based on sale prices after Club Card discounts. However, using manufacturer coupons does not have any effect on these purchase minimums. (This means thresholds are met after club card sale prices, but before coupons, whereas most CAT thresholds are before sale, before coupons.)
7. Internet printables must be scanable. They can be printed with black and white ink.
8. The highest value coupon presented for an item will be applied to the item, i.e., e-coupons.
9. Coupon Doublers vary by promotion and store, so ask at the individual store for answers to questions about their doubling policy.

Kroger

The Kroger Co. is the second grocery group to explore. The Kroger companies include: Baker's, City Market®, Dillons, Food4Less, Foods Co., Fred Meyer®, Fry's®, Gerbes®, Hilander, JayC, King Soopers®, Kroger®, Owen's, Pay Less, QFC, Ralphs®, Scotts, and Smith's®. The coupon policies

for all the stores are very similar and include only minor variances, but be sure to check with the actual store where you shop.

The Internet coupon policy for Smith's®, Kroger® and Dillon's is available online at http://print.coupons .com/Couponweb/Partners/Kroger/ Smiths/SmithsCouponAcceptance.html, and you can email Ralph®, Kroger, or Fred Meyer® for specifics about the regular coupon policy at their stores using the "contact us" links on their websites or call consumer affairs at 800.576.4377 for more information. You can load e-coupons to your "Plus Card" and also take advantage of

Catalina promotions. Ralphs doubles coupons, but you should be aware that Fred Meyer does not.

Important points in The Kroger Co. (particularly Ralphs) coupon policy are as follows:

1. Store and manufacturer coupons, Internet printables and e-coupons are accepted. (Store and Manu Qs can be combined on one item.)
2. Doubling Rules: manufacturer coupons worth $0.50 or less will be doubled; manufacturer coupons valued between $0.51 and $1.00 will be compensated at $1.00 value. Coupons over $1.00 do not change in value. (Fred Meyer does not double at all.)

3. Free or full-value coupons are limited to five per customer.
4. Coupons can't be used against "free" sale items.
5. Overage is not allowed and any coupon higher in value than the cost of the item will be adjusted down.
6. Internet printables must be scanable. They can be printed with black and white ink.
7. Free-item Internet printables are not accepted. Internet printables for 75% or more of an item's value are also not accepted.
8. Competitor Catalina coupons are accepted. (This means any cash register tape coupon, not just manufacturer Qs with other store logos.)
9. They do not accept competitor's transaction coupons, only item coupons.
10. Competitor pharmacy coupons accepted, but can't be used with the $4.00 Generic Program.

SuperValu

Stores in the SuperValu group include: Acme®, Albertsons®, Cub®, Farm Fresh®, Hornbacher's®, Jewel-Osco®, Lucky®, Save-A-Lot®, Shaw's/Star Market, Shop 'n Save, and Shoppers®. For information about Internet printable coupon policies, most are posted on the store's sites, such as the one for Shaw's (https://www.shaws.com/contact/faqs/coupons.jsp). To access Shaw's store coupons go to http://info.shaws.com/coupons/, and to access manufacturer coupons that pair with current weekly sales go to http://www.shaws.com/savings/viewcoupons, where you can click and add to your printable list. Coupon policies in this group can vary by retailer, area, district, and even store to store. Individual managers have final decision authority in coupon acceptance and limitations.

 The following points are based on Shaw's corporate policy:

1. Shaw's accepts store and manufacturer coupons, which can be combined for use on a single item.
2. Doubling Rules: manufacturer coupons $0.99 or less will be doubled, and compensated up to $1.98 in value. Coupons over $1.00 do not change in value. Only the first six coupons under $1.00 will be doubled. All others will be redeemed at face value. (Example: You can use ten $.50 coupons, but only the first six will double. The remaining four will be redeemed at 50 cents.)
3. Free- or full-value manufacturer coupons are accepted. Free coupons can be used with a BOGO sale.
4. BOGO Rules: BOGO coupons can be used with a BOGO sale. You can also combine a BOGO

manufacturer coupon and a BOGO store coupon for the same items. Shaw's® no longer accepts BOGO Internet printables.

5. Internet printables must be scanable. They can be printed with black and white ink.

6. Free-item Internet printables are not accepted. Shaw's does not accept Internet printables valued at $4.99 or more or any Internet printable valued greater than the cost of the item. Shaw's store Internet printables are limited to $10.00 value, cannot be doubled, and will be price adjusted to avoid overage, if needed.

7. Overage is not allowed, especially when pairing coupons, and any coupon(s) higher in value than the cost of the item will be adjusted down.

8. They do not accept CAT coupons from other stores but will accept manufacturer coupons for matching manufacturer items that have logos from other stores printed on them, only if they scan without beeping. (YMMV)

9. Competitor coupon acceptance varies widely; contact your individual store's customer service for more information.

SHOP ALBERTSONS?

In discussing the SuperValu group, I need to mention that there are really two Albertsons. One is part of the SuperValu group, but another, Albertsons LLC, is an independent retailer. If you live in Arizona, Colorado, Florida, Louisiana, New Mexico, or Texas you are likely shopping at the Albertsons LLC chain, and the coupon policies discussed as part of the SuperValu chain do not apply.

Off to the Supermarket!

Now you know all you need to know about store coupon policies to get you through the stores, so let's see just how I do it and how you can, too. It really is easy. Follow me:

1. Pick a store: Shaw's®, because they double Qs and offer CAT promotions.
2. Make a list: Break it down to three steps: basic weekly needs, your wants this week, and things you could use but could wait a week or so.

   A. Basic Needs

   Every week you have to buy certain items. (Okay, every other week if you shop less frequently.) Milk, bread, eggs, etc. I don't know what you generally want, but my list always includes milk, bread, eggs, bananas, hummus, and cheese. Just don't try to tell me your basic needs include mayonnaise, as one of my students insisted.

   B. Weekly (or bi-weekly) Wants

   These items are the things you are low on or just desire. Think about seasonal veggies and fruit. Proteins for suppers—that's "dinners" to those of you who live outside New England—and whatever foods you are in the mood for. Out of salad dressing? List it here. Planning on an Italian supper? Write down some pasta.

   C. Can It Wait?

   Buying these items isn't imperative and so you should only get them if they can be bought during a great sale, with a deal coupon, a CAT, or all three.
3. Note the Specials (Doublers/Store Qs/CATs/Special Sales): Quickly look over the flyer and see what, if anything, you should add. Is Cinco de Mayo next

week? You could pick up some tacos. Maybe avocados are on sale in a Ten for Ten; they would go great with those tacos. I call these add-on items, because they aren't part of the regular plan but go on your list because they work for you in accordance with the weekly sale. Add-ons are the part of the list that should only include a few items. For the most part, you already know what you need, so think of this as a bonus section to capitalize on CAT promotions and specialty sales.

4. Check the Q Databases: Here is the easiest part. It took a few minutes to write your list and another couple to look through the ad. Now go to your computer and pull up a coupon database. Enter the items on your list in the search bar and note any matches, printing those with links or marking those you'll have to cut out of inserts or magazines.

I actually type in every item, either by category or brand name. For milk, I type milk. For ketchup, it must be Heinz®. If I were catching the Cinco de Mayo sale I'd enter tacos, unless I noticed Ortega® was specifically on sale, for which I'd type "Ortega". Most coupons now are e-coupons or Internet printables, so once I click and print (or load), I'm pretty much ready to go. For the few that referred to paper coupons, I note it on my list. For example, Heinz coupons were in the *All You*, November 2010 issue. I'd note "(AY 11/10)" next to the word Heinz on my list. Only after all the paper coupons are noted do I bother to cut them out. While the last Internet coupons are printing, I grab my stack of inserts and magazines, and cut out those I just noted. Since there are usually only a few, the clipping takes only a couple of minutes. As for the Internet printables, I am far too lazy a couponer to waste time cutting neatly along the dotted lines. Instead I make a sharp fold and rip them as I walk to the car. Really!

5. STACK, STACK, STACK! With my list in hand and many coupons to use, I head off to the store, ready to stack as many as I can together, either with store and manufacturer coupons, or with the noted sales and CATs.

   If there are items I bought for free or as money makers that I know I don't want, like canned cat food, I usually drop them in the donation boxes at the exit of my local Shaw's. Then I don't even have to think about them later. And that's it. Shopping easily and quickly, with great discounts and minimal effort.

Should the process seem too overwhelming for you, develop your couponing skills in small doses. At first, don't worry so much about matching the sales and coupons; don't worry about CATs. Start by getting in the habit of using a coupon database before you head out. That's easy enough. In general, you have an idea of what items you typically buy. The next time, spend at least five minutes looking to match those items. Try not to do it too far in advance, because you'll lose the coupons or forget to use them. Instead, try allocating a few minutes before heading the store, as all the information will be fresh in your mind.

A second beginning step is actually holding back from shopping. You probably don't need half as much stuff as you typically buy. Spend a second to consider whether you need the item or not. A great deal of money is wasted on products you never intended to buy, but that's precisely what your supermarket wants you to do.

You can also use coupons for most home grocery delivery services. For example, Peapod—grocery chain Stop & Shop's delivery service—accepts online, Internet printable, and paper coupons. To access Peapod online coupons, click on the exclusive offers "Shop" button and add items to your cart from there, activating the coupon. Printed and paper coupons should be placed in an envelope and handed to the driver; Peapod will apply the coupon credits to your original payment form. (Remember to write your name and order number on the envelope.) Since Stop & Shop® is a doubling store, they also extend the doubling of coupons $0.99 and under policy to its Peapod home delivery service. The service is available in select New England areas.

Safeway, Genuardi's®, and Vons® home grocery delivery also accept coupons, though only those available online. Coupons loaded to the Club Card will apply as discounts if the card is registered and linked to your home delivery account, and is available in Arizona, California, Delaware, Maryland, Minnesota, New Jersey, Nevada, Oregon, Pennsylvania, Washington D.C., and Virginia.

In the spirit of grocery shopping, we should also discuss coupons use at U.S. commissaries. If you are part of a military family, you should definitely take advantage of commissary shopping. Not only do they offer extremely discounted prices and price-matching, but they accept manufacturer and military coupons, too. Printed internet coupons including BOGO Qs, though excluding free-item ones, are also accepted. While commissaries do not double or triple coupons, sometimes the exchange will offer doubling promotions where two regular coupons can be used against a single item. And remember, foreign overseas commissaries can accept expired coupons anywhere from one to six months expired. Best of all, look for those P&G inserts on the counter or ask someone to help. There really is nothing better than shopping at a store that accepts coupons and hands them out!

Healthy Coupons

Are organics a part of your lifestyle? Don't despair. These kinds of products do cost more than Cheetos®, but there are many ways to buy organic items with coupons. Two of my four family members are vegetarians, so I buy a lot of organic and non-meat products. Coming from a farming

family, I am also partial to fresh, local produce and animal-friendly meats and dairy. The first step you should consider as couponer with specific needs is writing to the organic and/or vegan companies whose products you favor. For example, I love Cedar's Hummus and we eat containers of it each week, so I am fairly loyal to Cedar's® products and download coupons from their website whenever I can. While I get my eggs from a local farm during the summer months, I also respect the way Eggland's Best treats their chickens and make sure to buy their eggs the rest of the year. Eggland's Best® regularly offers coupons to their consumers, especially those who are signed up for their mailing list. Finally, consider following couponing blogs that focus on organic items. For example, Organic on a Dime (http://organiconadime.blogspot. com/) is a great resource for organic shoppers as it covers specialty shopping for the following stores: Acme®, Earth Fare, Giant Eagle®, Harris Teeter, Marc's, Nature's Pantry, Whole Foods®, Mustard Seed, Target®, and Trader Joe's®. The site also offers links to organic coupons and other related deals. When printing organic coupons, keep in mind that they change quickly, so they should be printed as you find them.

If you or someone in your family has particular dietary needs due to medical issues or eating choices, planning may require a little more forethought, but not so much that it makes couponing difficult. The additional savings will offset a few minutes of extra prep, making your efforts worthwhile.

Shopping at farmer's markets is the best way to get fresh produce to your table. Locally grown produce and locally raised meat are generally healthier options. As items available at farmer's markets are better for the environment and better for you, most grocery-only shoppers think the prices are too high.

But you can find coupons and deals in farmer's markets, too. First, consider that a local grower may have a surplus if the growing season is particularly good, which results in a price decrease overall. Also, the fact that the markets are local keeps the farmer's travel and transportation costs down, which is translates into lower prices for you. Sometimes farmers will reward their loyal customers in transaction discounts or bonus items, further defraying costs. Do you regularly go to the farmer's market? Stay true to a few growers and ask for a discount.

All of these examples offset any additional costs of the fresh items. Also consider that local businesses regularly pass out coupons at farmer's markets. The farmers at the market where I live actually hand out "Mall Money," which are printed coupons valued at $1 to be used at the adjoining mall. Call or write to the U.S. Department of Agriculture and inquire about any farmer's markets coupons available in your area. You may be surprised.

Have you considered joining a **community supported agriculture (CSA)** program at a local farm? CSAs are a great way to get fresh, healthy, and sustainably produced food to your home by buying a share of the farm's crops or livestock. Are you or your spouse a veteran or currently serving overseas? Ask for a discount.

Maybe a share is too much for you, so ask for half-share or plan to split it with another family. What about a free trial share? Arrowhead Farm (www.arrow-headfamilyfarm.com), one of the country's oldest family farms just north of Boston, often offers a one-week free trial share to those who ask. You can always find ways to avoid paying out what is above your means; you just need to think alternatively.

Couponing is the start of thinking about purchases in a whole new way. Once you've mastered the first steps, you'll have the courage to apply the new perspective to other areas as well. If fresh, animal-friendly, and environmentally green foods are important to you, you can find a way to get them cheaper. You just have to ask.

READY FOR THE GROCERY GAME?

1. Typical item sales at grocery stores run on what cycle?
   a. 3–5 weeks.
   b. 4–6 weeks.
   c. 2–3 months.

2. You should buy produce ...
   a. In bulk.
   b. Only on sale.
   c. Seasonally.

3. What months are not associated with nationally sponsored foods?
   a. January, March, April, August, September, and December.
   b. March, April, August, September, November, and December.
   c. April, May, August, September, November, and December.

4. The two best ways to get a store's coupon policy do not include ...
   a. Emailing or mailing the corporate offices.
   b. Chatting up the customer service desk.
   c. Checking the store website, where many are posted.

5. Can Doublers be used with DND coupons?
   a. What are Doublers?
   b. Of course!
   c. Not a chance!

6. The best way to capitalize at grocery stores is to combine which of the following?

  a. Coupons and special sales.

  b. Special sales and CATs.

  c. Coupons, special sales and CATs.

7. The easiest way to grocery couponing is to use what?

  a. Q databases and Internet printables.

  b. E-coupons and loadable loyalty cards.

  c. Farmer's markets.

8. Ralphs®, Dillon's®, and Fred Meyer® are part of which larger grocery affiliation?

  a. The SuperValu group.

  b. Safeway Inc.

  c. The Kroger Co.

9. The second section of your grocery list should be the ...

  a. Basic Needs.

  b. Weekly Wants.

  c. Can It Wait?

10. Shopping at farmer's markets and for organics and animal-friendly products ...

  a. Requires a little more forethought and planning.

  b. Is too hard; don't bother.

  c. Is nothing that interests my family.

Answers: 1. b, 2. c, 3. c, 4. b, 5. c, 6. c, 7. b, 8. c, 9. b, 10. a

Links to a few store policies:

Giant®: http://www.giantfoodstores.com (click "savings," then "coupons," then "coupon policies.)

Hannaford®: http://www.hannaford.com (click on "about hannaford," then "FAQs" on the left-hand side, then scroll to the bottom of the page for coupon info)

Kroger®/Smith's®: http://print.coupons.com/Coupon-web/Partners/Kroger/Smiths/SmithsCouponAcceptance.html

Meijer®: http://custhelp.meijer.com/app/answers/detail/a_id/92/~/what-is-the-meijer-store-coupon-policy%3F

Safeway: http://www.safeway.com (click on "Our Store," then click "coupon policy" on the left-hand side under "Related Links)

Shaw's®:https://www.shaws.com/contact/faqs/coupons.jsp

Stop & Shop®: http://www.stopandshop.com (click "Customer Service" at the bottom of the page, then "FAQs" and look under "Other Popular Topics)

Vons: http://www.vons.com/ifl/grocery/Coupons-Policy

Check out www.lazycouponer.com for more links to up-to-date policies.

CHAPTER 7

Redefining Drugstores

CAN I GET A "WOO-HOO"? THE EXCITEMENT OF beginning the drugstore chapter is almost too much for me. I never considered drugstores a source of any real value until I became a couponer. Drugstores are not just pharmacies; they are where you should expect to buy all your personal and household items. Need Tide® or Windex®? Go to a drugstore. You need razors or feminine products? Go to a drugstore. Diapers or shampoo? Drugstore. Sunscreen, paper towels, candy, or toys? Again, drugstore! Toys? Yes, I said toys—I'll give you a great example from my recent shopping.

Just before my son Derek's birthday, I was at CVS® and noticed Bumblebee, a *Transformer*, in the toy section. Derek was obsessed with *Transformers* at the time. He had Transformer sheets and a comforter, Transformer costumes, talking masks, and coloring books. We own the entire Transformer series on DVD and, if I let him, he'd sit watching it all day. However, he had no Transformer toys. (He was only three, and those toys are difficult to manipulate.) Anyway, Bumblebee is his favorite Transformer, so I knew I had to get it. Why not go to **Toys"R"Us® (TRU)**?

Here's why. Bumblebee was $14.99 at CVS and $11.99 at TRU, but stacking coupons at CVS is much easier; I knew I could get it cheaper there. I grabbed a Gillette® razor for

$9.99 (earning $6.99 ECBs), which worked for me because Gillette razors are the only ones my husband will use. I brought both the razor and Bumblebee to the register, where I used a $5/$20 transaction Q, a $6.00 Gillette manufacturer Q, a $4.00 Gillette Video Values Q from Rite Aid® (my CVS accepts competitor Qs) and spent only $9.98 out of pocket (OOP) for both items, which was still cheaper than Bumblebee alone at TRU. In addition, I actually earned $6.99 in ECBs, so my final price for the beloved Bumblebee? $2.99!

The same principle that governs shopping at grocery stores applies to drugstores. Pick one, any one, and master it first. Then you can take on whichever competitors reside around the corner. This chapter covers the three major drugstore chains—Walgreens, CVS®, and Rite Aid®—their loyalty cards, rewards programs, rebate programs, and policies. I will also show you to read their flyers, earn coupons through Rite Aid®'s Video Values program, and navigate through the iheart websites for each one, giving you sale previews and related coupon links. You might think at the outset that the prices at drugstores are too high, because you remember seeing the same products for less at supercenters, but a large percentage of drugstore savings comes from shopping there repeatedly. Each of these three major drugstore chains rewards frequent shoppers with their rewards programs. They also generate coupons specific to you and your shopping habits as based on your loyalty card purchases. Overall, drugstore items only appear to cost more, but with scenario-building and smart couponing, most of what you'll get will be free. Yes, that's right, FREE. Don't believe me? What about that drugstore run I wrote about in the Introduction? Did you forget it already? There's more to come.

Walgreens (Wags)

To be honest, I am not a big **Walgreens (Wags)** shopper because the closest Wags is located in the next town over and I am far too lazy to drive the ten minutes it requires to get there. (I told you that I was lazy. Did you really doubt me?) However, Walgreens is the largest national drugstore chain and it is coupon-friendly. So, depending on where you live, it could be a great shopping opportunity for you. Here are the important points of Walgreens's coupon policy:

General:

1. Wags accepts store and manufacturer coupons. A MQ can be combined with Walgreens in-ad coupons from the circular. Overage during a transaction is not allowed, and any coupon(s) higher in value than the cost of the item will be adjusted down.

2. Store personnel can limit the number of identical coupons and the quantity of bulk item purchases by a single customer within a day at their discretion. (Relationships, relationships, relationships.)

3. BOGOs—you can use up to two manufacturer coupons (one for each item) in a BOGO sale or one BOGO coupon, making both items free. You cannot combine the both types and overage is not allowed.

4. Internet printables are accepted and can be printed with black and white ink.

5. Wags does not accept expired or competitor coupons.

Register Rewards (RR):

6. Earning: Items must be in stock during their promotion. There are no substitutions. Only one RR is printed per offer for a transaction. If you use an RR on a qualifying item, you will not earn the additional

Register Reward.

7. Using: Wags does not accept expired RRs. No over-age is allowed and the Register Reward will be modified if used against a lesser-priced sale item. You cannot use more RRs than items purchased. If an item on which a Register Reward was used is returned, the RR will not be refunded to the customer. RRs can't be used on gift cards, pre-paid cards, tobacco, alcoholic beverages, dairy products, lottery tickets, money orders, transportation passes, event tickets, or postage stamps.

Walgreens is probably best known in the coupon world for their in-ad coupons. Walgreens circulars, covering sales Sunday through Saturday, usually include in-ad Qs that differ from most other stores because the Wags Qs actually determine the sale price.

Without the coupon, you must pay whatever the list price is. For example, if the Good Start® formula pictured here regularly costs $24.99, you will have to pay $24.99 unless you bother to hand the cashier the coupon during checkout. (If you forget, there's a stack of flyers by the door!) These Wal-

greens coupons can absolutely be stacked with manufacturer coupons for greater savings, as long as the amount of coupons used is not greater than the number of products bought. If you want to shop Walgreens regularly, you'll have to utilize fillers in order to achieve the maximum savings there. For example, if I were to buy the Good

Start® formula using the above in-ad Q, I'd have to add another item to my transaction if I also want to use a manufacturer coupon with it. Then, I would purchase the formula, a filler (pack of gum), and use the Wags Q and a Good Start MQ, reaching the best discount possible. (This is also a bit too much effort for me and another reason I don't shop Walgreens.)

Wags is also known for its **Register Rewards (RR)** program. Register Rewards are actually Catalina Marketing promotions printed On Your Next Order (OYNO) coupons on cash register tape (CRT). Suppose you see Colgate toothpaste advertised in the Wags circular for $2.29, with a $1.50 Register Reward and you happen to have a $1.49 manufacturer coupon for Colgate®. The initial purchase of the toothpaste and use of the coupon would only cost $0.80 out of pocket, and you'd earn a $1.50 RR, meaning you would earn $0.70 on your purchase! Since Walgreens is a true CAT store, problems concerning the printing of RR should be addressed to Catalina Marketing at coupon@catalinamarketing.com or by calling 1-888-8coupon and choosing option 3.

Finally, Walgreens has in-store coupon booklets. Wags offers both seasonal coupon booklets and children's activity booklets that are filled with store coupons. If you don't see them as you walk in, ask the cashier or check the pharmacy.

 ## CVS/pharmacy®

CVS is the second-largest drugstore chain, supporting some 7,000 stores and offering the largest retail rewards program nationally, with over 66 million active cardholders. While CVS doesn't post their coupon acceptance policy online, you can inquire about it by contacting Customer Relations at 1-800-SHOP-CVS or by mailing your request to CVS Corporate Headquarters, One CVS Drive, Woonsocket, RI 02895.

Their general coupon acceptance is as follows:

1. CVS accepts both store and manufacturer coupons. (They can be stacked together for a single item's purchase.)
2. Only one transaction coupon or **offer at the register (OAR)** coupon per transaction. (These are the coupons that CVS mails or emails you, which are not earned by making purchases—like ECBs—but instead are randomly generated, and are sometimes linked to your loyalty card as an ExtraCare member.)
3. ECBs: You can use more than one Extra Buck coupon provided the purchase threshold has been met for each offer amount on a per-transaction basis. For example, if you purchase one item for $10.00 and have three $3.00 ECBs, you may use all three in the transaction, because ECBs are considered to be like cash, not coupons. They should be used after coupons and if lost, they are not usually replaceable.
4. BOGO: You can use one manufacturer's BOGO coupon, getting both items free or you can use two manufacturer's coupons for a specific dollar amount off. You cannot combine BOGO Qs with other MQs. (Stores can set quantity limits to BOGO purchases.)

5. CVS® does not permit overage. If the register beeps, cashiers must price-modify coupons to match the item price.
6. Internet printables are accepted but they must properly scan because CVS does not allow manual overrides at the register for printed Qs.
7. CVS sometimes accepts competitors' and expired coupons, but the policies at each store can vary. Check at the store level about their practices.

CVS runs their sales Sunday through Saturday, sometimes with special one- or three-day sales at the beginning of the week. Circulars include in-ad coupons, information about CAT-like promotions, and what items earn ExtraCare Bucks (ECBs).

ECBs, which are CVS® store money, are the rewards earned by purchasing eligible items during the promotion period and printed on cash register tape. CVS's ExtraCare program is linked to your loyalty card, so you have to get one before you can access their ExtraCare rewards. You can get your own ExtraCare card by going to your local CVS store or by signing up on www.cvs.com. Click the ExtraCare tab, then the "Sign Up" link. You can also register your card there by clicking the "Attach an ExtraCare Card" link and entering your card number and email. Though registering your email online with your ExtraCare card is not necessary to receive ExtraCare Buck rewards, doing so will generate additional personalized coupons to your email inbox.

Once you have your ExtraCare card, you are ready to earn rewards, which can happen one of two ways:

quarterly or instantly. Quarterly ECB rewards are earned automatically when the cashier swipes your card during checkout and are paid out to you each quarter—January, April, July and October 1st—at the bottom of your transaction receipt on or following the pay out date. It can be earned by email if your card is registered online. The program earns 2% of dollars spent for every non-prescription purchase and $1 ECB for every two prescriptions bought. (Certain restrictions apply regarding prescription-earning rewards in NJ, NY, and LA, as well as with prescriptions purchased using state supplemental health plans.) You can also check your quarterly ECB status online. Not only does CVS reward you with ECBs for every purchase you make using your ExtraCare Card, but they also track your purchases so shopping more earns ECBs for the items you actually want.

The second way to earn ECBs is instantly. The easiest way to get instant ECBs is to scan your ExtraCare card at the price-check kiosks in the store. Simply hold the backside of the card so that the red light scans the barcode, then transaction and item coupons and special offers will print from the side, as pictured here. (Reaching in and giving a gentle tug if they get stuck in the machine usually loosens them.)

The other way you can get instant ECBs is by purchasing items that qualify for rewards. ECB reward-earning items are advertised in the store, marked with signs hanging near the products, or within the weekly circular. ECBs earned by buying trigger-ing products are generated as dollar amount CRTs, more like store cash, and should be given to the cashier after all your coupons are scanned. Many items throughout each week are **"Free with Extra Bucks" (FEBs)**. That means the purchase price of the item will be printed as an ECB reward on your CRT. If you are really clever, you could pair a FEB item with a manufacturer coupon to make the best use of the deal.

For example, imagine looking through the flyer and you see this advertisement for ThermaCare® heat wraps. Notice the sale price for the item reads $2.79 and the Extra Bucks earned for purchasing it are also $2.79, making the item free.

However, you know to check the Q databases by now, so you look up ThermaCare and dis-cover the following $1.00 Internet printable that you can use when you purchase the product. Your ExtraCare rewards then are $1.00 higher in value than you actually paid out of pocket, making you money. CVS® is a great place for new couponers to first realize money makers!

Like every other store you shop, begin your couponing at drugstores by following the technique:

1. Pick a store, 2. Make a list, 3. Note the specials, 4. Check a Q database, and 5. Stack, stack, stack!

EXTRACARE NOTES

1. Limit one ExtraCare card per person.
2. ECBs have expiration dates, so remember: use them or lose them!
3. ECB promotions may run weekly or monthly.
4. Most ECB rewards have a "Limit 1" notation, meaning that you may only receive one ECB regardless of how many of the corresponding products you buy during the offer period. Check for limit restrictions so you can maximize your savings.
5. On transaction threshold earning ECB promotions, such as spend $25 get $5 ECBs, the purchase amount is determined by the after-sale, pre-coupon price.
6. You can use as many ECBs to pay for products as you have. However, if the total ECBs you use exceed the purchase price, you forfeit the difference. (For example: if you use $3.00 in ECBs to pay for $2.50 worth of items, you lose $0.50.) I suggest you grab a filler instead of losing the money, like a pack of gum or candy bar.
7. Any trouble printing ECBs should be handled by a store manager or through calling the ExtraCare program at 1-800-SHOP-CVS.

Remember this example where I turned $32.96 of product into an $10.96 money maker? (see page 97) Now, let me walk you through it. The store was easy: CVS®. Next, I wrote down what I wanted: a newspaper. So that is it for me. I wanted to buy my Sunday paper and I refused to spend money doing it, so I checked the special promotions to see how I'd get it free this week. (I mean really, should you really have to pay for coupon inserts? I don't think so.) As with any store, a quick read of the flyer allowed me to note the specials, particularly the FEBs—or close to free—and BOGO sales. Then I noted any matching coupons. Here's what it looked like:

Free with ECBs

    Aussie® Shampoo, Conditioner, or Styler $2.99
        Get $2 EB (Limit 1)
    –$1 Aussie Product (RedPlum 02/14)
    Colgate® Total® Advanced Toothpaste 4 oz $2.99
        Get $2 EB (Limit 1)
    –$1 Colgate Total Toothpaste (4-oz.+) (*All You* Jan 2010)
    Crest® Pro-Health Toothpaste $3.50
        Get $3.50 EB (Limit 2)
    –$.75 Crest Toothpaste 4 oz+ or Liquid Gel (P&G 2/7)
    –$1 MQ from Crest Sample Pack

BOGO Items

    SoBe® Life Water 20 oz BOGO
    –SoBe Lifewater 20 oz BOGO Internet Printable (up to $1.50)

Fillers

    CVS Tissues $.99
    Cat Litter $.99
    Candy $.50–$.99
    Newspaper YMMV (the item I actually wanted!)

After noting the specials and checking the databases for matching Qs, I go about heading to the store to stack, or combine as many of the special sales, promotions and coupons together, as I possibly can. In this case, it was actually cheaper for me to get extra items, so I bought all the FEB items and added the BOGO SoBe drinks to donate and some cat litter and tissues for my house. Notice the cost differences between the two possible transactions, the first with FEB only items, the second with extra products.

Transaction of Free Items Only:
$2.99 Colgate® Toothpaste
$7.00 Crest® Pro Health (2)
$2.99 Aussie® Product
= $12.98 subtotal
−$2 (2) Crest $1/1Qs
−$1 Aussie Q
−$1 Colgate Q
−$6.94 ECBs I had in my wallet
= $2.04 OOP, earned $11 ECBs ($2 Aussie,
        $2 Colgate, $7 Crest)

Transaction with Additional Items (My Actual Purchase):
$12.98 Aussie, Colgate, Crest (2)
$1.98 CVS® Tissues (2)
$1.98 Cat Litter (2)
$5.60 SoBe® (4)
= $22.54 subtotal
−$5/$20 CVS transaction
−$1/2 CVS® tissues
−$2 (2) Crest® $1/1Qs
−$1 Aussie Q
−$1 Colgate Q
−$5.60 (2) SoBe® BOGO Qs
−$6.94 ECBs I had in my wallet
= $0.04 OOP, earned $11 ECBs

Notice with the second transaction I actually saved an additional $2.04 because the extra products boosted the transaction total high enough to use a $5.00/$20.00 transaction coupon. When you start off, try to build scenarios like the first one, but as you consistently realize success and ease in stacking, add in additional items to turn your savings into greater amounts.

When you first start to coupon at CVS, the couponing community encourages you to build ECBs by making several small transactions and "rolling" the rewards between transactions. In other words, you buy a few items, earn the ECBs, then make another purchase right on the spot to earn more ECBs. (It is the same technique most suggest for Wags Register Rewards, too.) I used, or rolled, $6.94 in ECBs in my transaction, but only because they were already in my wallet. However, I advise you not to bother breaking up transactions in order to build ECBs. That is just that kind of over-thinking that over-exercises your mind and makes couponing tedious. And, sometimes it's not even to your advantage. If you regularly shop at CVS, you'll usually have some ECBs around. Whenever I earn ECBs, I wrap them around my ExtraCare card before returning them to my wallet. When I am ready to pay, the ECBs are right there for me to use. If I don't have any, it's no big deal because I'll generate more another time.

Remember the items I just showed you that cost me four cents OOP and earned $11.00 in ECBs? Well, here is what your transactions would look like if you followed that "rolling" advice:

Transaction 1

$2.99 Colgate®

−$1.00 Colgate MQ

= $2.00 OOP, earns $2.00 in ECBs

Transaction 2

$2.99 Aussie®

−$1.00 Aussie MQ

−$2.00 ECB earned from transaction 1

= $0 OOP, earns $2.00 in ECBs

Transaction 3

$3.50 Crest®

−$1.00 Crest MQ

−$2.00 ECB from transaction 2

= $.50 OOP, earns $3.50 in ECBs

Transaction 4

$3.50 Crest & $1 Filler

−$1.00 Crest MQ

−$3.50 ECB from transaction 3

= $0 OOP, earns $3.50 ECBs

After the four transactions, you'd pay $2.50 OOP and earn only $3.50 in ECBs. Is a dollar really worth standing in line and going through four transactions? No way! Besides, you would make more ECBs by buying the items in one transaction, paying $8.96 OOP and earning $11.00 in ECBs—a $2.00 gain. Also, I don't believe rolling with multiple transactions is in the spirit of intended ECB use, so think about using fillers instead.

Another misconception is that you need to be totally prepared before you shop, chasing all sorts of deals. I promise you it isn't the case. Of course you'll fare better with a little prep, but the process doesn't have to be all that complicated to still do well. Coupons are to help you save money, not upset the balance of your work and personal time. Let me illustrate how a good couponing deal can still come about with minimal prep (five minutes) and a legitimate need (I was out of toilet paper and trash bags). Though it's not a money maker, I think it is a great example of major savings in just a few minutes' time. Here goes:

Pre-Sale Total

$210.36

My Total

$19.89

I really was on my way to CVS® to buy some toilet paper and trash bags because I was almost out of toilet paper and totally out of trash bags. I also intended to grab one of the Oral-B® electric tooth-brushes if they were in stock, because I'd been waiting to get one for my husband and had a rain check for two. Before I left for the store, I quickly scanned the flyer and saw that Proctor & Gamble was offering a "Spend $20, Get $5" promotion. Since we only use Charmin® at my house and it's a P&G product, the deal worked into my needs well and I added a package of Bounty® to my list. Then I remembered my four-year-old wanted Santa to leave him soft tissues, so I added Puffs® to my list. (Yes, he was serious about this request.) All those items were P&G products and they qualified for $5.00 back in ECBs. Finally, I grabbed $3.25 worth of P&G coupons and left for the store.

CVS RAIN CHECKS

CVS issues rain checks for both sale items and ECB promotion items. If your store is out of stock, just ask the cashier for a rain check. They will give it to you along with the date, item description, ECB code, and re-ward.

When I got to the store, I remembered it was **Friends and Family (F&F)** day, where using an F&F coupon took an extra 30% off non-sale items. I was only buying sale items, so I ignored it. Then I walked over to the price scanner machine and scanned my loyalty card, where it printed out a $4.00/$20 coupon and another coupon for $30.00 off a Craig portable television/DVD player, because they had some on sale for $99.99. I wasn't really interested at first until I thought about my other son, who was home sick. Maybe he'd like to watch a movie in bed. (I don't allow TVs in the kids' rooms.) So I went over to the portables and noticed one 7" DVD/CD combo player. I price-checked the DVD player and it scanned at full price of $82.99, because it was an older packaged model. Next I approached the manager, Hannah, and asked her for a F&F 30% coupon to use on the DVD player; I also asked for last week's Holiday book, in which there was a scanable coupon

earning $4.00 in ECBs if you spent $20, which now I was going to do.

The CVS® Holiday book is a booklet advertising the special products and sales offered November and December. It always includes an ECB earning transaction coupon.

Then I checked the toothbrushes and they had two, so I picked them up as well. Next to the toothbrushes was an end-cap filled with lip balm, and as I walked by I noticed an unadvertised sale that made the EOS lip balm free, so I added one to my cart, grabbed my

P&G items and trash bags, and headed to the register. Here is how it played out:

$6.88 Bounty® 8-roll (reg. $9.99)

$3.88 (4) $.97 Puffs® (reg. $1.99 each)

$10.66 (2) $5.33 Charmin® 12-roll (reg. $9.29 each)

$46.00 (2) $23.00 Oral-B® Floss Action Recharge Toothbrush (reg. $32.99 each)

$2.99 EOS Lip Balm (reg. $3.49)

$82.99 7" Craig Portable DVD/CD Player

$8.99 Hefty® EZ Flap 80 ct Trash Bags

$10.15 MA tax based on 162.39 (reg. $12.38, based on taxable $197.98)

scanned the 4/20 Holiday Book Q earns $4 ECBs

= $172.54 subtotal (reg. priced $210.36)

–$30 DVD CVS Q

–$20 @ (2) $10 Oral B Q

–$4/$20 CVS Transaction Q

–$1 $1/2 Charmin Q

– $.25 $.25/3 Puffs Q

–$2 Bounty Q

–$27.60 @ 30% off non-sale F&F Q applied to trash bags and DVD player

–$6.04 ($4.11 actual MA State tax adjusted from 10.15 for after Q prices)

–$23.77 in ECBs in my wallet

= $57.88 Out of Pocket

–$37.99 ECBs earned via scanned Holiday Q gets 4.00 ECBs, P&G S$20G$5 CAT gets $5.00 ECBs, Oral-Bs get (2) $13.00 ECBs, EOS lip balm gets $2.99 ECBs

= $19.89 Final Cost

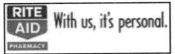

Rite Aid® (RA)

Below is my Rite Aid® run of 02/14/10, with a **PSP (pre-sale price)** of $86.00.

My total:

I earned $4.41 in cash back and a $100 P&G Coupon Book = Major Money Maker!

How did I do this? Simple. Let me walk you through it. First, you'll need to know Rite Aid®'s coupon policy. Here are the most important points:

1. RA accepts store and manufacturer coupons. A MQ can be combined with coupons from the RA circular that say manufacturer coupon on them. They can also be combined with AdPerk (Video Values) coupons.
2. Overage during a transaction is not allowed, and any coupon(s) higher in value than the cost of the item will be adjusted down.
3. Store personnel can limit the amount of identical coupons, the number of transaction coupons, and the quantity of bulk item purchases by a single customer within a day at their discretion. (Again, build-

ing relationships by knowing staff is key.)

4. BOGOs—you can use only one manufacturer coupon on a BOGO sale. You may not use a BOGO coupon. Overage is not allowed.

5. Internet printables greater than or equal to $5.00 are not accepted. Rite Aid® store coupons printed off the Internet are not subjected to the $5.00 limitation. All printable coupons can be printed with black and white ink.

6. Transaction Coupons (TQs)—Manufacturer coupons used with TQs are deducted after the total purchase price has been decided. (This means you give the cashier your TQ first, then the other coupons.) Also, you may use more than one TQ at a time, as long as you break the transactions up and each meets the threshold requirement.

7. Rite Aid® does not accept expired coupons. Check with your local store about competitors' coupons: YMMV.

RA STORE OR MANUFACTURER Q?

Remember, coupons with a single barcode with the "RC" before the numbers are store coupons. RC is Rite Aid's code for coupons, and therefore can be stacked along with manufacturer coupons. Also, any coupons with barcodes beginning with a 48 are Rite Aid store coupons. Even if a coupon says Manufacturer's Coupon, any RC-coded coupon is actually a store coupon.

Rite Aid® is the third-largest drugstore chain in the U.S., covering 31 states. Except the southern California stores, which run their ads Friday through Thursday, Rite Aid® sales cycle go Sunday through Saturday. Rite Aid®'s circular also includes in-ad coupons, UP Rewards, Video Value, and Single Check Rebate match-ups.

Suppose I need Pepto-Bismol®. I know it is on sale at RA this week for $2.99, and upon checking the flyer I see a $2.00 in-ad Q. I  also remember seeing $1.00 Pepto MQs in my "A Year of Savings" Proctor & Gamble coupon booklet, which I quickly confirm by checking a Q database. Stacking the $2.00 RA in-ad Q (it's barcoded RC) and the $1.00 Pepto MQ (adjusted down to $0.99 by the cashier) will allow me to purchase the $2.99 product for free, further settling my tummy with my smart little shopping victory.

I really love to shop Rite Aid® because it is the only store where you can earn actual money, not money coupons, but real take-it-to-the-bank money. I always begin RA shopping by looking through the flyer to find the items that are free or close to free with in-ad or AdPerk Video Values coupons or the Single Check Rebate program. Single Check Rebates (SCR) is Rite Aid®'s rebate program that you can access through the mail or the Internet. Don't worry: it's not difficult at all. There are only two rebates I ever bother to take advantage of. The first is the one where you mail a receipt to Proctor & Gamble showing $25.00 worth of purchased products, and they'll mail you "A Year of Savings" coupon booklet. The other is Rite Aid®'s SCR program.

Every month, Rite Aid® releases an SCR circular, called the Rebate Directory, outlining each of the month's many rebates and defines the time period in which the products must be purchased. Sometimes you must buy the items on a single day, most times within a sales week, and sometimes over an entire month or quarter. Be certain you

check the promotion date because SCR deals have been known to run the last week of a month to the second week of the next month. Because the flyer tells you all this information in great detail, you can use it as a guide for needed coupons you intend to use later in the month. It's like a heads-up for the really good freebie sales, because a huge portion of the items are free after reimbursement from the SCR program. You can also access rebate information online at

https://riteaid.rebateplus.com/.

SCRs are not connected to your Wellness loyalty card. Rather, they are linked to information on your in-store or

online receipts.

Either fill out the form on the back of the Rebate Directory, as pictured here or go online to https://riteaid.rebateplus.com.

For online orders, you'll need to enter the order number, date and time of purchase, and for in-store transactions, you'll be required to

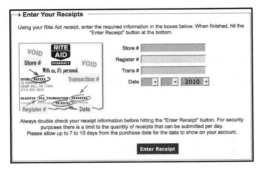

provide the store and transaction numbers and date and time of purchase from your receipt in order to be reimbursed for qualifying items.

Rite Aid® will then send you an actual check in the mail.

They look like postcards and can be cashed at your bank. SCR checks are mailed out within a week of the request and are limited to one per household. However, if you shop, say, for an elderly family member, they can have rebates sent to them at their home as well. Should you be savvy enough to use a coupon against a **Free after Rebate (FAR or Freebate)** item when you purchase it, you'll actually get paid to buy it.

For example, Dove® Men+ Care Body and Face wash was on sale for $4.00 with a $4.00 SCR. It would be listed in the Rebate Directory by date and offer number. Here the

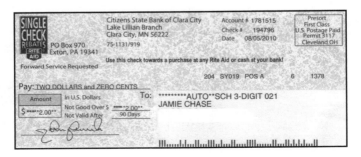

FAR Dove® Men+ Care is Single Check Rebate offer #52. Additionally, there were two coupons available for the product, one at $1.50 and the other $1.25. So, if you were to use the higher-value coupon against the product when purchasing it, you'd pay only $2.50 out of pocket and would get back $4.00, making $1.50 in the deal. Stacking Rite Aid® transaction coupons against FAR items is also a great way to earn money. Suppose you stacked a $5.00/$25.00 TQ on a purchase of completely FAR items, you'd pay $5.00 less out of pocket than Rite Aid® would reimburse you through the SCR program. What is better than getting paid to shop for stuff you already need?

NOT SO LAZY?

Rite Aid does offer rain checks for sale items if they are not in stock. I suggest keeping a copy of the ad with the rain check for later reference. If it is a Single Check Rebate item, send the copied ad and the receipt, noting the "rain check adjusted purchase price" to Rite Aid Single Check Rebates via fax at 1.800.457.2243 or mail to P.O. Box 8340, Wilmington, DE 19803, along with your contact information and specifics about the SCR. They will credit your account or send out an additional SCR check.

By either looking through the weekly sale flyer or monthly rebate flyer, I make note of the items that are free or close to free with SCR, and check the Q databases for any matching coupons. Here is how I'd write it out:

Free with SCR
> Dove® Men+ Care Body & Face Wash 13.5 oz, $4, get $4
> SCR #52 *Overage with Q
> –$1.50 Dove® Men + Care Body and Face Wash IP

–$1.25 Dove®Men + Care Body Wash or Scrubber (V 1/31)

Notable SCRs

Gillette® Shave Gel $2.24 (Special Sale)

–$1/1 SCR #53

–$1/1 Gillette Shave Gel (P&G 2/7)

Vicks® DayQuil® or NyQuil® $3.99

–$1/2 SCR #15

–$2/1 Vicks DayQuil® or NyQuil® (P&G 1/17)

Next, I scan the flyer for good sale items to use with

AdPerk Qs. AdPerk coupons, also known as **Video Values** (VV) Qs, are Rite Aid®'s printable store coupons that you earn by watching little video advertisements on the AdPerk site (http://my.AdPerk.com/).

You must log on to the AdPerk site and select the video you want to watch. The videos are no more than a short commercial, gener-ally 15 seconds to two minutes, which you choose from the many Video Library offers for products ranging from food to medicine to toys and always including an extra coupon good on any product. Just click on the product picture and the video will begin.

A time-progress bar will display, and you'll immediately know how long the video is, making it easy to watch while

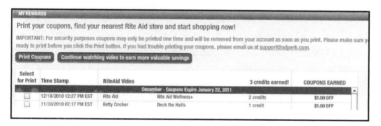

doing something else. I play the AdPerk videos when I am making dinner, because I don't have the time to give it my full attention. Before becoming a parent, I'd watch the Video Values during television commercials, but when do I ever have time for TV nowadays? Now cooking supper doubles with video watching, making it all super easy.

After viewing the video, a code pops up that you must enter within 30 seconds in order to access the coupon.

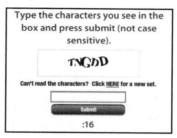

Type the characters you see in the box and press submit (not case sensitive).

TNGDD

Can't read the characters? Click HERE for a new set.

Submit

:16

If you haven't already done so, you'll need to login to your Video Values account and go to the "My Rewards" tab, where a screen will pop up showing

MY REWARDS

Print your coupons, find your nearest Rite Aid store and start shopping now!

IMPORTANT: For security purposes coupons may only be printed one time and will be removed from your account as soon as you print. Please make sure you are ready to print before you click the Print button. If you had trouble printing your coupons, please email us at support@adperk.com.

Print Coupons   Continue watching video to earn more valuable savings

Select for Print	Time Stamp	RiteAid Video		3 credits earned!	COUPONS EARNED
		December - Coupons Expire January 22, 2011			
☐	12/18/2010 12:27 PM EST	Rite Aid	Rite Aid Wellness+	2 credits	$1.00 OFF
☐	11/30/2010 07:17 PM EST	Betty Crocker	Deck the Halls	1 credit	$1.00 OFF

the coupons you've earned.

Click the square next to the coupon description and then the "Print Coupons" button at the top of the screen, which will give you a store coupon to stack along with a manufacturer coupon for

the product you are purchasing at Rite Aid®.

After looking through the flyer for good VV matching deals, I note them like this:

Free with AdPerk

> Carefree® Ultra Pantiliners 16 ct $1.99
> –$2/1 AdPerk Carefree 01/10
> –$1/1 Carefree® Product, 28 ct+ or Carefree® Ultra
>   Protection (V 1/3)
> Stayfree® Pads 28–48 ct $1.99
> –$1 AdPerk Stayfree 02/10
> –$1 Peelies on some Stayfree Packages or IPs
> Post® Shredded Wheat, Grape Nuts, or Raisin Bran
> $1.75
> –$2 Post Shredded Wheat, Grape Nuts, or Raisin Bran
>   IP

Next, I look for anything free or close to free with UP Rewards (UPs). UPs are the cash register tape rewards you get for purchasing pre-established items that trigger the reward.

UP rewards are linked to your Wellness card, much like CVS®'s ECBs and their ExtraCare Card, except at Rite Aid®, the loyalty card earns you a percentage off every transaction based on the points you've earned and your member status level. Details regarding member levels and savings are pictured here:

EARN POINTS EVERY TIME YOU SHOP

- Earn one point for every dollar spent on non-prescription purchases.[1]
- Earn 25 points for every prescription you purchase.[1]

MEMBER LEVEL*	POINTS	REWARDS
plus	for every 125 points[†]	a one-time, 10% off shopping pass[2]
silver +	500 points	10% off all non-prescription purchases every day[3] free health screenings[4]
gold +	1,000 points	20% off all non-prescription points purchases every day[3]

*All members are enrolled at the plus level and can earn their way to silver+ and gold+.
[†]For every 125 points up to 375.

PLUS, ENJOY EVERYDAY BENEFITS, INCLUDING:

- Members-only sale pricing throughout the store
- 10% off Rite Aid Brand products every day[5]
- 24/7 exclusive access to a pharmacist when you call 1-800-RITEAID

You can first sign up for Rite Aid®'s Wellness card either online or at the store. Either way, you'll need to register the card at www.riteaid.com/wellness in order to start receiving its benefits. Once registered, RA will send you a $5/$25 OYNO transaction coupon as a thank-you, so you better be prepared to stack well and use it to its fullest!

TO PRINT OR NOT TO PRINT

With AdPerk Qs, you don't actually have to print the coupons right away, since they are good for two months and stay in your My Rewards list until you print them. I try to watch the videos in the first few days of the month and print them only before I leave for the store, when I print other coupons I find on the databases. That way, they are fresh in my hand, I don't have to file them, and they're less likely to get misplaced.

Normally, I would note any good UP deals and matching Qs, but since there were none available for the transaction (photo on page 166), I went to the final steps of listing any other good CATs, Sale/Q Match-ups, and reasonable fillers for the transaction. In this particular case, they were offering a Proctor & Gamble "Buy $25.00 worth of products, get $5" (B$25G$5) where you could earn a Visa card instead of an OYNO coupon or UP.

The remaining noted specials are as follows:

CAT: (P&G)
B$25G$5Visa, B$50G$15Visa, B$100G$35Visa

Notable Q Match-ups

$7.99 Venus® Razor
–$2.00 Venus Razor (P&G 2/7)
Puffs® Tissue $0.99
–$0.99 Puffs (Free) WYB 2 Vicks® products (P&G 2/7)
Olay Body Wash $8.99
–$8.99 Olay® Body Wash (Free) wyb Venus Razor (P&G 2/7)

Fillers

RA Paper Plates $1.00
Cat Litter $0.99
Holiday Candy 50% (Mars®/Dove® have SCR)
Newspaper YMMV

Since I had two different transaction coupons and also wanted my Proctor & Gamble products listed separately to mail in for my P&G *Book of Savings*, I broke the products into two transactions.

Transaction 1:

$1.98 Cat Litter (2)

$5.98 Dove® Valentine Hearts (2)

$1.75 Post® Grape Nuts

$4.00 Dove® Men's Body Wash

$3.98 StayFree® (2)

$7.96 CareFree® (4)

$1.98 RA Plates (2)

= $27.63 + $.08 tax (subtotal)

-$5.00 $$5/$20 RA VV Q

-$2.00 $1/1 StayFree MQ (2)

-$2.00 $1/1 StayFree VV Q (2)

-$4.00 $1/1 CareFree MQ (4)

-$8.00 $2/1 CareFree VV Q (4)

-$1.00 $1/2 Dove Chocolates MQ

-$1.00 $1/2 Dove Chocolates VV Q

-$2.00 Post Grape Nuts IP

-$1.25 Dove Men's Body Wash

-$1.00 $1/2 RA Plates, Cups, or Tissues

= $0.46 OOP, earns $5 SCR

Transaction 2:

$7.99 Venus® Razor

$8.99 Olay® Body Wash

$7.98 Vicks® DayQuil®/NyQuil® (Buy 2)

$0.99 Puffs® Tissues

$2.24 Gillette® Shave Gel

= $28.19 + $0.42 tax (subtotal)

-$5.00 $$5/$20 RA VV Q

-$8.99 Olay Wash (Free) wyb Venus Razor

-$1.50 Venus Razor (P&G 2/7)

-$4 (2) $2/1 Vicks (P&G 1/17)

-$0.99 Puffs (Free) wyb 2 Vicks

-$1 Gillette Shave Gel (P&G 2/7)

= $7.13 OOP, earns $2 SCR & $5 Visa

The total for both transactions, totaling 19 items, was $0.46 + $7.13 = $7.59 out of pocket, and I received a $7.00 check for reaching the SCR and a $5 Visa gift card from RA, as well as the $100 P&G coupon book! By using coupons in combination with Rite Aid®'s several rewards programs—Wellness discounts, UP Rewards, Single Check Rebates, and AdPerk (Video Values)—it is easy to see how Rite Aid® is a valuable resource for couponers.

Finally, Rite Aid® offers a special program to seniors at least 60 years old (62 in New Jersey) that includes 10% off cash prescriptions and Rite Aid®–brand products. It is a free loyalty card obtained at the pharmacy. In addition, membership earns 10% off most all products purchased on Tuesdays and information about unadvertised sales. As a member, you also receive a quarterly *Living More* newsletter that customizes articles and coupons based on your purchases. You can access the newsletter online, though it can also be mailed if requested. (Seniors residing in California should check with their pharmacy about additional restrictions.)

Iheart Websites

One final way to easily build scenarios and learn about drugstores is made super easy through checking the iheart websites. These sites, www.iheartwags, www.iheartcvs, and www.iheartriteaid.com, detail each store's current week's sales and matching coupons as well as show information for a couple of weeks in advance so you can be on the lookout for matching Qs ahead of time.

They also offer a great deal of information on properly shopping the drugstores and changes to each store's coupon policy. For store-to-store information on coupon policy as detailed at the iheart sites, check out these links. http://www.iheartwags.com/2010/08/wags-official

coupon-policy.html

http://www.iheartcvs.com/2008/12/cvs-coupon
guide.html

http://www.iheartriteaid.com/2009/10/official-rite-aid
coupon-acceptance.html

STILL THINK THEY'RE JUST PHARMACIES?

1. Where should you buy your personal care and household items?

a. Grocery stores.

b. Supercenters.

c. Drugstores.

2. Where did I find the Bumblebee Transformer cheapest?

a. Toys"R"Us.

b. Walgreens.

c. CVS.

3. Which is the largest drugstore chain?

a. Walgreens

b. CVS.

c. Rite Aid.

4. Who offers the biggest loyalty card program?

a. Walgreens

b. CVS.

c. Rite Aid.

5. Walgreens's Catalina Marketing program is called ...
   a. Register Rewards.
   b. ExtraCare Bucks.
   c. UPs.

6. CVS's loyalty reward program is called ...
   a. Register Rewards.
   b. ExtraCare Bucks, linked to the ExtraCare card.
   c. UPs, linked to the Wellness card.

7. Rite Aid's loyalty reward program is called ...
   a. Register Rewards.
   b. ExtraCare Bucks, linked to the ExtraCare card.
   c. UPs, linked to the Wellness card.

8. At what store can you earn actual money back?
   a. Walgreens
   b. CVS.
   c. Rite Aid®.

9. Which URL is not an actual iheart website?
   a. www.iheartcvs.com
   b. www.iheartwalgreens.com
   c. www.iheartriteaid.com

10. What information is not available at iheart sites?
    a. Viewing current and advanced flyers.
    b. Matching coupon links and coupon policy information.
    c. Account information linked to your personal
       loyalty card.

Answers: 1. c, 2. c, 3. a, 4. b, 5. a, 6. b, 7. c, 8. c, 9. b, 10. c

CHAPTER 8

Navigating Supercenters & More

EVER FEEL LIKE A HERDED SHEEP WHEN YOU'RE out shopping? That's how many of us feel inside a supercenter. Supercenters and mega-chains tend to feel overwhelming, and that's why you have to learn how to shop properly at them. Key elements to successful saving include awareness of price-matching policies, sales and flyers, coupon use and limitations, acceptance of competitor coupons, loyalty cards, and email lists. In this chapter, we will explore stores like Walmart®, Target®, Kmart®, Kohl's®, and Toys"R"Us®. With some insider savvy, you can beat their everyday low prices.

Here, I'll provide you with the details regarding coupon and price-matching policies, and all the really important stuff that makes shopping at each store unique. I'll also show you what you should be looking for while shopping there.

Finally, this chapter will take you into the area of web shopping, including directions to the best options for online coupon codes, like Retail Me Not. As a bonus, I will also discuss a few Freebie sites and show you how to obtain all those wonderful samples that come in the mail, usually with Qs inside!

Walmart®

Since Walmart is the biggest of the super- stores, we'll start there. Walmart numbers almost 4,000 stores in the United States alone, and nearly 3,000 of those stores are Supercenters. Many people are surprised to find out that I rarely shop at Walmart, but that's because Walmart doesn't offer Catalinas, gift card promotions, or loyalty card benefits. While Walmart offers a pretty flexi- ble corporate coupon policy, people in certain locations find consistent resistance in coupon shopping there. So your success as a Walmart customer using coupons depends on how assertive you are, the coupon-friendli- ness of your nearest Walmart, and your knowledge of its corporate policy. Until you have built relationships and experience regular success coupon shopping there, I sug- gest you always carry a copy of their corporate coupon policy to guide both you and the cashier. In May of 2011, Walmart made coupon-friendly changes to their corpo- rate coupon policy, which is available online at http:// walmartstores.com/7655.aspx.

Important points in Walmart coupon policy are as follows:

1. Store and manufacturer coupons and Internet printa- bles are accepted. (Store and Manu Qs cannot be combined on one item.)
2. Walmart accepts free or full-value coupons, though not IPs.
3. BOGO coupons are accepted as long as maximum price is specified.
4. Walmart accepts pharmacy coupons and soda caps where permissible by state law.
5. Internet printables must be scanable, have remit-to addresses, expiration dates, and explicitly say

"Manufacturer Coupon" on them.

6. They do not accept expired coupons.
7. One coupon per item only. There is no limit to the number of coupons used per transaction.
8. If you have 40 or more coupons, a coupon valued at $20 or more for a single item, or coupons used in one transaction totaling $50 or more in value, you'll need approval from management ahead of time.
9. Walmart gives overage if the coupon value exceeds the item price in the form of cash or as a discount applied to remaining items within the transaction.
10. Competitors' coupons are accepted, but not competitor transaction Qs.*
11. Competitors' Catalina Qs for specific items with "remit to" addresses are accepted.
12. Black-and-white coupons are absolutely accepted at Walmart.

*Different Walmart locations may have different practices on competitors' coupons. The Walmart nearest me refuses to accept them while friends in other areas (as close as twenty minutes away) have great success using competitors' coupons at their nearby Walmart stores. If you are planning to use competitors' coupons, I suggest you first check with that particular store's management.

NOT ONE FOR ALL

Walmart's limit on coupons per purchase means one coupon per item you purchase, not one coupon per transaction. If you are buying three boxes of tissues and have three $.30/1 coupons, you may use all of them. If your store's cashiers have trouble with this concept, be certain to carry Walmart's coupon policy with you when shopping, as the policy clearly states, "Only one coupon per item is permitted."

Besides the many coupons Walmart accepts, they also will price-match competitor ads. Competitor ads must be for the current week and regular types of sales, therefore excluding promotions like "Holiday before 5 a.m." sale pricing or "Spend $20, get $5" (S$20G$5) promotions. The ad must be for a retail store, not an online store, and presented in the original format on which it was printed. Also, the item must be exactly the same as featured in the ad and in stock at the time of purchase.

WALMART PRICE MATCHING

Should you want to price-match an item at Walmart, simply inform the cashier of your desired price match and show him the original matching competitor's ad before he begins to ring it up. The process is very simple and can be completed right at the checkout registers, unlike at other stores where you are required to first go to the customer service desk.

Supercenters are only a portion of the Walmart operations. Discount Stores, Neighborhood Markets, and their online site www.walmart.com round out the package. In particular, Walmart.com is a great way to shop for products, especially large items you can't get in any local stores. By using their free Site-to-Store shipping, you can get oversized items delivered to a nearby Walmart for free. For example, if I were to order a small couch online at walmart.com, the cost of freight to my house would be $49.95, but delivery to the nearest Walmart store—a ten minutes' drive—is absolutely free. Site-to-store shipping is a wonderful added value to already discounted prices.

Walmart does not distribute a regular weekly ad or coupon insert, but you can find many coupons online at

InStoresNow http://instoresnow.walmart.com/In-Stores-Now-Coupons.aspx) or through Walmart's *All You* magazine, which you can order by subscription or buy at your local store.

Without the various specialty promotions—like a GC (gift card) or CATs—the only way to really make out at Walmart is to match your coupons with the "Roll Back" sales they offer. Since Walmart stores dot the entire U.S., most of the previously discussed coupon blogs such as West Coast's KCL (http://thekrazycouponlady.com), Georgia's ThriftyMama (http://www.thethriftymama.com), and New England's HTSFF (http://www.howtoshop

forfree.net), as well as other couponing blogs, cover Roll Back and coupon match-ups nearest them. On the site, look for the Walmart tab to find the deals. Don't forget, Walmart® pricing and sales are regional, so YMMV (your mileage may vary) depending on the store. If you seek Walmart deal match-ups, I would stick to coupon bloggers in your area.

Finally, if you are interested in receiving free samples, consider checking out Walmart's free sample site (http://instoresnow.walmart.com/In-Stores-Now-Free-Samples.aspx). You don't have to sign up for membership to access the free samples; rather, click on the sample you want sent to your home and enter your mailing address and email. Usually with the sample offer appears a box you may check to receive a free email subscription to the Walmart Wire.

Also check instoresnow.walmart.com for the "Value of the Day" and free events in your area like product demonstrations and food or beverage samplings.

Target®

Target®, the second largest of the mega-chains, is very coupon friendly. Target® also offers gift card promotions, price matching, and store coupons. Target®'s coupon policy is available on their corporate website www.target®.com (Click Coupons at the bottom of the page under "Target® Stores," then click "Target® Coupon Policy" on the left-hand side of the screen.) You can also print it from kiosks inside the store.

Target®'s policy is very plain, and the most relevant points are summarized here:

1. Target® accepts store and manufacturer coupons, which can be combined on a single item unless either coupon explicitly says otherwise.
2. Target® accepts Internet printables, and they can be printed in black and white ink.
3. Target® does not give overage on coupons, and cashiers are expected to price-modify a coupon's value if it exceeds an item's cost.
4. They do not accept competitor's coupons.

Target® offers the easiest way to print coupons through www.target®.com/coupons, where you can print both manufacturer and store coupons. The best part about this site is that while most coupon sites limit your printing to two of each coupon, you may print as many Target® store coupons as you want.

TARGET OR MANU Q?

Coupons printed off the Target coupon link will display Target logos on them no matter whether they are manufacturer or store coupons. Make sure you read the actual coupon so you know how to properly stack them. Target store coupons say "Target Web Coupon" on the top, and manufacturer coupons that Target suggests be used at Target stores say "Manufacturer Coupon" on top. Further, when the coupon shows both the Target Bullseye and the word Target underneath, it is a store coupon, whereas coupons that show the Target Bullseye without the printed word Target are manufacturer coupons. Also, a triple barcode means MQ, and a single barcode is only for SQs. And don't forget, if the coupon contains an address for the retailer to send the coupon back to the manufacturer, then it is definitely a MQ.

Target® also offers many gift card promotions. Though not true Catalinas, they work much the same way—you purchase certain items, then they trigger a gift card (instead of the more typical OYNO coupons). Sometimes couponers refer to these promotions as GC CATs instead of GC promotions. If you are clever in combining gift card CATs with store and manufacturer coupons for the items you buy, you may end up making money in the process. For example, suppose Target® is offering a $5.00 gift card promotion for Pantene® shampoo, regularly $5.84, when you buy two. You check the Target® coupon site and find $2.00/1 store coupons for Pantene shampoo that you can combine with the $2.00/2 Pantene products manufacturer coupon you found in the P&G (Proctor and Gamble) insert. When you arrive at Target®, the sale price for cheapest qualifying shampoo is $4.75. (You know this because you scanned the shampoo's barcode in the price-checker machine at the end of the aisle, and it confirmed the sale price and the item's inclusion in the gift card promotion.)

Here is what the transaction would look like:

Bought
$9.50 Pantene® Shampoo (2)
Used
–$2.00 Pantene MQ
–$4.00 Pantene SQs (2)
Subtotal = $3.50 OOP, earns $5 GC
= +$1.50 Money Maker

Target® also price-matches a competitor's printed ads. You can check the details and exclusions regarding Target®'s price-matching policy online

(http://sites.target®.com/site/en/company/page.jsp?
contentId=WCMP04-040400).

The basics of the policy are as follows:
1. Target® stores will match printed, local, and current
   ads or catalogs showing the identical product and
   quantity.
2. Price matching applies to items already purchased if
   the current ad and receipt are brought to the service
   desk within seven days of purchase.
3. Ad photos, photocopies, cell pictures, or torn ads
   will not be honored.
4. Ads must be from a like-competitor in the same area
   and cannot be for timed, holiday, percent-off, loyalty
   card, close-out, or clearance events.
5. You may use coupons with price matching.
6. Manu Qs apply after price match.
7. Target® store Qs apply before price match.
8. If stacking both, the order in which you should present coupons is SQ/price adjust/MQ.

Using coupons along with Target® price-matching is
easy and can be done at any register or at the customer
service desk. It is so incredibly easy that Target® is the only
place I have ever bothered to price-match. Below is an
example of a Christmas-time Target® price match I did
against a Toys"R"Us® Buy one, get one at 50% sale—where
I also used both store and manufacturer coupons. The
LeapFrog® Leapster® games were on sale at Target® for
$15 each, and I had a $5.00 off $30.00 Target® store
coupon on Leapster games and two $5.00 off one Leap-
ster game manufacturer coupons.

Here is how this transaction played out:

Bought

$30.00 Leapster® games (2)

Used

–$5.00 ($5/$30) Leapster Target® Q

–$7.50 Price Toys"R"Us® price match—B1G1@50%

–$10.00 (2 @ $5/1) Leapster MQs

= $7.50 OOP for (2) Games, a 75% savings!

Target®.com and the retail stores have different policies. Target®.com does not offer price matching and Target® stores do not price-match any online prices, including those for items at target.com. However, target®.com will price-adjust an item bought online if the item appears at lower price in the Target® Weekly Ad from one to seven days from the time of ordering and if you contact them during the week of the ad. (Clearance items are excluded for price adjusting.)

Speaking of clearance items, Target® is known for their amazing clearance and markdown pricing. As Deal Seeking Mom's blog (http://dealseekingmom.com/target®/) points out, Target® has a national markdown schedule running on a two-week cycle until general products reach 75% off and Holiday up to 90%. The markdown days are as follows.

Monday: Children's clothes, electronics, and stationery

Tuesday: Domestics, grocery, pet products, and women's clothes

Wednesday: Health and beauty, lawn and garden, men's clothes, and toys

Thursday: Books, decor, housewares, lingerie, luggage, movies, music, shoes, and sporting goods

Friday: Automotive, cosmetics, hardware, and jewelry

POST-HOLIDAY MARKDOWNS

Holiday markdowns usually happen in a 3, 3, 2 day pattern, with the percentages taken by the following guidelines:

50% off within first three days
75% off from days four to six
90% off on the seventh or eight days
(Note: Christmas markdowns vary slightly because of the massive stock.)

If checking the markdowns doesn't appeal to you because, like me, you are too lazy to bother to wait, consider the last gem that Target® offers its customers: trial sizes! Target offers a comprehensive supply of travel products, usually tucked neatly in a corner at most Target® stores. Since the variety of products offered is so large, Target is known throughout the couponing world for them. One friend did her family's laundry for six months using sample-sized All® detergent she picked up for free at Target. Many coupons apply to trial-size items, but be certain your coupon doesn't explicitly say, "Excludes Trial Size." If the coupon says "Good on Any Product," it definitely can be used for trial-sized products.

For instance, if you had this Nexcare™ bandage coupon, you could use it on trial-sized Nexcare products, since it doesn't exclude them. The little Nexcare packages usually sell at Target® for $0.99, so this $1.00 coupon would beep and need to be manually price-reduced to the value of $0.99 by the cashier; the item is still free, though. While you may not want to spend half a year using tiny detergent

bottles, a few Nexcare bandages probably last as long and are worth grabbing next time you are at the store. See, lazy can be smart, too.

Other super-coupon-friendly services Target® offers are coupons texted to your smart phone, and assistance with coupon-use, should you encounter a problem. To get the scanable coupon images texted to your phone, sign up on Target's website. You can access the page by going to www.target.com and typing, "Mobile coupon" into the search bar. Mobile Target store coupons are just like any other store coupons and can therefore be stacked with manufacturer Qs. For more about Target's mobile couponing, including a new app. go to www.lazycouponer.com. For coupon assistance, simply call 1-800-440-0680 while in the store, and the Target® Guest Relations Team will help you and the store's retail managers resolve any issues!

Kmart®

Kmart, a national chain with more than 1,300 stores, includes under its umbrella Big Kmart, Kmart Supercenters, and regular Kmart stores. In the world of couponing, Kmart is known for doubling promotions. As many as 10 coupons can be doubled, as high as $2.00 in value up to $4.00 each. The store offers doubling events regularly, but your area's participation is usually quarterly. For some stores, the event may only be offered twice a year, while others may have one every other month. Check your Kmart's weekly ad to see if your store is participating. Look for the "Double Manufacturer Coupons" box on the front of the circular. Kmart® doubling promotions are linked to their loyalty card, so you must have a loyalty card to benefit from them.

DON'T STOP AT 10

double manufacturer's coupon event up to $2!

Most of Kmart's doubling events limit the coupons to 10, but you can still use as many as coupons as the store allows. For example, if I present 14 coupons to the cashier during the promotion, the first 10 coupons will double and the remaining four will be credited at face value.

You can obtain Kmart's free loyalty card in the store or online at kmart.com. Simply access the loyalty card page and click the "Earn Today and Join Now" button. Since Kmart is part of the Sears Corporation, you can use your loyalty card at Sears®, Kmart, Lands' End®, and online at kmart.com, sears.com, and mygofer.com, where you earn one percent back on your purchases by getting 10 points for every $1.00 you spend.

Their loyalty card program is called Shop Your Way

Rewards, and points can be redeemed at stores or online. Also, each time a cashier scans your card, you will have a record of the purchase should you need to return or exchange the item later, so you don't have to hold on to the receipt. Card use also generates CRT (cash register tape) coupons personalized for you, many even for free items.

Though Kmart® is a coupon-friendly store, they do not post a corporate coupon policy on their website. Therefore, if you have a specific coupon question, you can email corporate customer service and they'll be able to answer it. They generally do not, however, forward complete policy information on anything other than the doubling events. Instead they answer individual questions as received. Through frequent shopping at Kmart and information compiled over time with my coupon buddy, I can offer the following guidelines, but urge you to email customer service directly to find specific answers pertaining to your area Kmart.

Here is the gist of the Kmart's coupon rules:

1. Kmart accepts MQs, BOGO Qs, FVCs, and SQs with few restrictions except that they must scan properly.
2. You cannot combine store and manufacturer coupons on a single item. (Sadly, no stacking!)
3. Internet Printables must scan properly and should not exceed 75% of the item's value (though YMMV with this one).
4. Kmart does not give overage for coupons, and they use Smart registers that automatically adjust any coupon's value down to that of the selling price.
5. Store managers and cashiers have some discretion regarding what their store allows, so make sure you know both the staff and individual store well.

Kmart®, much like Target®, offers an online coupon center to print store and manufacturer coupons, though most store coupons are usually ones that pertain to loyalty card use and building rewards points. Go to kmart.com (http://www.kmart.com; click the "Kmart Deals" link at the bottom of the page, then click "Coupon Center") to access these coupons. Also like Target®, Kmart has an extensive trial size collection, so check out items like bandages, detergent, toothpaste, and wipes. And, like Walmart®, Kmart offers free shipping to Kmart stores on most products ordered through their Mygofer website.

As for Kmart's sales cycle, it begins Sunday and goes through Saturday.

You can pick up traditional circulars or sign up for text or email about sales specials or promotions online. (http://www.kmart.com; click the "Kmart Deals" link at the bottom of the page, then click "Sign up for email savings!")

KOHL'S

Kohl's®

Kohl's is a national department store chain with over 1,000 stores. It is best known for their constant store coupons, credit card member rewards, discounts, and its $5.00 email registration coupon. Go online to kohls.com (just click the "today's ad" link at the top under the search bar) to view the weekly ad in your area or to sign up for their email alerts. If you haven't already, make sure you do sign up because Kohl's will send you a $5.00 off coupon to use on anything except the charitable dolls and books near the register. They will also email you a 10% coupon code off your next online order at kohls.com, where shipping is only $0.99 per item!

PLAYING BY THE RULES

Just because something is available online doesn't always mean it is ethical to use it. I know many couponers encourage the "purchase" of Kohl's® $5.00 coupons from Internet sources for as little as $1.00 for 20 coupons. Please remember that Kohl's distributes these coupons to legitimate email addresses for the intention of encouraging your future shopping with them and as a thank-you for joining their email list. That said, if you and your spouse have separate emails, I encourage you both to sign up, giving you two usable coupons. As long as you both view the ads, I believe it is within the spirit of Kohl's program.

Once you join Kohl's email list, you'll be offered many different Kohl's coupons each week, sometimes multiple coupons within a few days. Kohl's is wicked awesome—it has to be written somewhere; I am from Boston—about their constant stream of store coupons, from dollar-off to transaction percent coupons to discount shopping passes to online coupon codes! Kohl's® simply offers the best variety of store coupons. While you get some coupons through signing up for emails, also join the list while at the store so more will be mailed to your door. Should you have a Kohl's credit card, too, you'll be exposed to even more coupons as part of their loyalty rewards.

The best way to shop Kohl's is to take advantage of their various coupons and mix them with whatever specialty sale Kohl's may be running, from "Back to School" to "Early Bird" or "Night Owl" to holiday specials or to their weekly sales. Also remember that Kohl's regularly offers a huge selection of clearance items, for which they accept those Qs!

 ## Toys"R"Us®

Toys"R"Us is the first place that comes to mind when thinking about children's presents. Servicing eight countries with an enormous variety, Toys"R"Us is a great place to get toys. Also, Toys"R"Us is wonderful about coupon use, so I urge you take a look at it through a couponer's eyes. Just keep in mind that supercenters like Walmart or Target® or even drugstores can surpass it in value and available discounts, if shopped right.

Toys"R"Us does not give out an official coupon policy neither online nor in response to requests, but their customer service will answer any couponing questions you have. Simply contact 1-800-ToysRUs.

The summary of a discussion I had with their customer service representative regarding policy is as follows:

1. Toys"R"Us® accepts manufacturer coupons and store coupons from either Toys"R"Us or Babies"R"Us.
2. They accept BOGO Qs, Full Value Qs, and Internet Printables with the only specified restriction that IPs must scan and "look" legitimate.
3. IPs printed in black and white are acceptable and there is no set value limit to them.
4. Both "R"Us family stores accept smart phone coupons—iPhone and Android—if the registers are updated and able to scan them.
5. Babies"R"Us® coupons that say "for a Baby Product" refer to items used for children under nine months of age.

Toys"R"Us does post their Toys"R"Us and Babies"R"Us Rewards Program, linked with their loyalty card. You can access information about the program by going online to either Toys"R"Us or Babies"R"Us and clicking the "Rewards"R"Us Link" link, or by going directly to

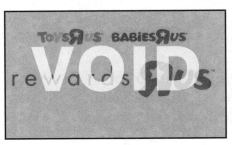

http://rewardsrus. toysrus.com/. There you can read about the program or enroll online by clicking the "Enroll Here" link at toysrus.com/rewards. You must make a pur-chase using your loyalty card to activate it. You may also enroll inside a store, where you must follow up registration online at toysrus.com/rewards by clicking the "Register Here" link.

Once you join, you will earn a $5.00 rewards certificate for every $150.00 in qualifying purchases, up to $20.00 per month. They are called "R"Us Dollars. Toys"R"Us® also offers diaper rewards to card members: you earn one Value box of Huggies® or Pampers® for every nine boxes of the same brand, as well as formula rewards.

THE FORMULA FOR REWARDS

Here is some useful information from ToysRUs.com. For all of these offers, you must be a member and you must make the purchases within a 12-month period:

1. Get one free Gerber® Good Start case of 32 oz. Ready-to-Feed Infant Formula for every 9 Gerber Good Start 32 oz Ready-to-Feed Infant Formula cases purchased.

2. Get one free Similac® case of 32 oz. Ready-to-Feed Infant Formula for every 9 Similac 32 oz. of Ready-to-Feed Infant Formula cases purchased. Offer valid for Similac Advance, Similac Sensitive and Similac Soy Isomil only.

3. Get one free Enfamil™ case of 32 fl. oz. Ready-to-Feed Infant Formula for every 9 Enfamil 32 fl. oz. of Ready-to-Feed Infant Formula cases purchased.

4. Get one free can of Babies"R"Us Infant Formula Powder 23.2 oz. or larger for every 9 cans of Babies"R"Us Infant Formula Powder 23.2 oz. or larger purchased.

Also, Rewards"R"Us members can earn a free LeapFrog book or game for every four purchased, and/or a free American Greetings® card for every five bought. Rewards for the above four specialty rewards come in the form of certificates rather than "R"Us dollars. Rewards members also receive benefits such as advance sale details, member-only shopping events, exclusive email discounts and coupons, and product recall information. I personally feel it is one of the most comprehensive loyalty card programs, as effective as those offered by the major drugstore chains.

If you have children under 10 years old, I also suggest signing up for the Geoffrey's Birthday club: http://www.trubdayclub.com/. Then he or she will receive a birthday card and gift—and a call if you desire—from Geoffrey the Giraffe to your home. Also, if you bring your child to a Toys"R"Us® store on their birthday, he or she will get a birthday crown, balloon, and a birthday announcement over the loudspeaker. Kids think it is great fun!

Freebie Coupon Code Sites

This book would not be complete if I didn't point you toward a few sample sites besides http://instoresnow.walmart.com. Walmart's free samples are the easiest to get if you are not comfortable with computers because the site is so easy to navigate. The Walmart® corporation also offers free samples to Sam's Club® members through the Daily Insider at http://www5.samsclub.com/Daily Insider.aspx. All you need to do is to enter your address and Sam's club membership number.

One of my favorite freebie sites is http://thefreebie blogger.com/. Here you can find all sorts of things from free samples to music downloads to Chuck E. Cheese's® tokens. The site also provides links to what is free with coupons at various stores nationally.

The other, and my true favorite, is MySavings

(http://www.mysavings.com/free-product-samples-section/), where you can find the largest range of free samples from many sources. To get some of the samples, you must fill out your address, while other manufacturers require you to answer a few questions, which I am always too lazy to do. However, mysavings.com compiles so many freebies, it takes only seconds to have a ton of them coming your way.

CAUTION!

With Free Sample and Freebie Sites you may want to stick to only one or two, because each time you enter your info you can't be sure where it goes or with whom it is shared. Also, I suggest you never join one where you must sign up with the blogger in order to access the information. Plenty of sites generate money through advertisements rather than selling your information.

To close this chapter, I'd like to remind you about finding coupon codes before you checkout at online stores. Remember sites like www.retailmenot.com and www.behindthe counter.com/, where you can find some of the best online coupon codes. If you do nothing else when shopping online, open up another tab in your browser and go to one of these sites. For Retail Me Not, just type in the name of the website from which you are ordering, like www.barnesandnoble.com. For Behind the Counter, you need to click the store's tab, such as for Home Depot® or Kohl's®, to see the codes. You can also type "(Store Name) Coupon Code" into the Google™ or Bing™ search bars if that's easier for you. Any of those ways you choose, I think you'd be surprised at how many results you generate. Then additional savings is just a click away!

FEELING SUPER?

1. Which of these Supercenters does not post its coupon policy online?
   a. Kmart®
   b. Walmart®
   c. Target®

2. The second largest Supercenter is ...
   a. Kmart
   b. Walmart
   c. Target®

3. One coupon per purchase means what?
   a. You may only use one like coupon each visit.
   b. You may only use one like coupon per transaction.
   c. You may use one coupon per each item purchased.

4. Which one of the following do both Walmart and Target not have?
   a. Price-matching policies
   b. Loyalty cards
   c. Internet posted corporate coupon policies

5. Walmart's couponing magazine is called ...
   a. *All You*
   b. *The Walmart Wire*
   c. *In Stores Now*

6. What is the right order when couponing with Target's price match policy?

a. Target® coupon, competitor price match, manufacturer coupon

b. Target® coupon, manufacturer coupon, competitor price match

c. Competitor price match, Target® coupon, manufacturer coupon

7. Target® is best known to couponers for their ...
   a. Gift card promotions
   b. Markdown and clearance items
   c. Trial size selection
   d. All of the above!

8. The Shop Your Way Rewards card is good where?
   a. The "R"Us companies
   b. Kmart® only
   c. Kmart®, Sears®, Lands' End®, and Mygofer

9. Which of the following is not a reward offered through the Toys"R"Us® loyalty card rewards?
   a. "R" dollars, LeapFrog®, and American Greetings® cards
   b. Hasbro™ games and Matchbox® cars
   c. Baby formula, Pampers®, and Huggies®

10. My favorite freebie/sample site is?
    a. instoresnow.walmart.com
    b. thefreebieblogger.com
    c. mysavings.com

Answers: 1. a, 2. c, 3. c, 4. b, 5. a, 6. a, 7. d, 8. c, 9. b, 10. c

CHAPTER 9:
Making Time Work for You

EVERY JANUARY, LOADS OF PEOPLE MAKE A New Year's resolution to save money through using coupons. By February, most of them have given up. When I ask why they quit, they always reply, "It takes way too much time." If I try to tell them that couponing doesn't have to take much time at all, they make an excuse like, "Well, I work full-time and simply don't have the time you do."

I couldn't force people to listen to me on how easy couponing can be, so I decided to teach a class. That class led to some local media coverage, which led to a lot of media coverage and eventually this book. And, since you are reading this book, I already have your attention. So, I'll start this chapter by making an extremely important point. Couponing is really easy if you know how to effectively manage your time!

The first step in learning how to manage your time wisely is not to get stressed and overwhelmed, as so many new-bies do. Planning your time well, both before and during your shopping trips, will help you avoid this pitfall. As a newbie couponer, you can avoid becoming bogged down by remembering one simple rule: There's always another sale. Seriously, life is too short to worry about every sale. You missed one sale? Another one is coming up in another week or two. Relax.

Let's look at an example of self-defeating behavior. Margaret is the type of shopper who drives everywhere for a deal. One Black Friday, Margaret called me to brag about all the money she saved on her Christmas shopping. She drove through two states, she informed me, and she and her shopping buddy shopped at fourteen stores. It is true that Margaret saved an average of 45 percent on all the products she purchased, but that doesn't consider all the driving costs as well as the several hours of her time she spent in the car. When all the factors are added up, Margaret invested too much time and costs to justify her monetary savings. She would have been better off covering fewer stores and planning her time better.

The moral? Don't worry about catching every sale and using each one of your coupons. There is always another sale and another coupon on the horizon. If you constantly chase sales, you'll end up spending all of your energy on searching websites, reading flyers, and running around chasing store specials. You can probably save a few dollars more by doing that, but how much money do you spend on gas to achieve it? Further, how much is your time worth? I value my time and am not willing to lose two hours a day to the sales chase. Even if my weekly savings increased by an additional $50, I would never give up so much personal time. And you shouldn't either.

Please don't misunderstand. Coupons have contributed greatly to my family's overall lifestyle, including both savings and, for me, an income stream, but let's get real.

Coupons have been around a long time. People have been using them since Coca-Cola® first introduced the concept in 1887. By the Depression era, coupons had become relatively common. Today, coupons pop up everywhere, offered by manufacturers, by stores, and even by government agencies. I can't remember the last time I bought anything without a coupon, other than my sons' preschool. (Even for that, however, I was sure to ask for a discount.) Instead of wearing yourself out to maximize each and every cent, pull back and allow yourself the freedom to catch the deals you can and take joy in those deals you do find.

Let's go back to the extra weekly savings of $50 for running yourself ragged while chasing sales. After you subtract the gas, printer ink, and electricity spent on the computer, you'd only being making $4.50 or less an hour for your time. Aren't you worth more than that? Yes, you are. So truly consider the amount of time you spend couponing.

I do all my couponing preparation for the week in fifteen to twenty minutes. That's right: fifteen to twenty minutes per week. My weekly drugstore run takes about another fifteen to twenty minutes on top of the time spent shopping, and the additional time the cashier takes at the grocery store to ring in all my coupons is probably about five minutes. So that's it: forty-five minutes or less in a week and I am done. If I miss something, oh well. I'll find another win some day and maybe you'll find the one I missed.

LEARNING TO BREATHE

Recently, I taught an older student, Donna, who had trouble with her time management and constantly felt paralyzed by couponing. In our first class, Donna claimed to spend between one to two hours each day trying to coupon. When I asked her why she spent so long and what she thought she actually accomplished, she answered, "Nothing. I am mostly frustrated." Donna had tried to coupon several times before and got overwhelmed. She took my class to get past the frustration and save money without feeling as though she was working a second job. My first suggestion to Donna was: Breathe. "It's just couponing," I reminded her.

The only time I allocate more time to couponing is during the holiday season between Thanksgiving and Christmas—actually, the week before Thanksgiving to the week after Christmas. Even then, I limit my minutes, keep my life in control, and my time in check.

When starting off, it is very important that you set a strict time limit. In the end, the time spent preparing isn't what leads to your overall success. The practice and expertise acquired over each week as you get to understand the coupon world is by far the biggest factor in saving.

Preparing for Success

At first, couponing may take you a little longer, so I would set a reasonable time limit of thirty to forty minutes a week to find coupons and deals and another twenty minutes for organization and clipping. Even if you haven't completed checking all of the sales flyers and coupon sites in that time, stop and go with what you have. You won't save much more money even if you keep looking for another hour. Instead, you'll just exhaust yourself and eventually give up.

Remember, the big savings will come when you gain more experience. Limit your coupon prep to one hour total. One hour, then stop. Anything more and you might spiral into coupon mania. After a while, you'll begin to notice trends and be able to prepare yourself in advance. Also, you will gain additional time-savings once you learn the smart way to collect and print coupons.

Many new couponers waste a lot of their time overprinting coupons. That creates a tremendous amount of waste, both in time and supplies. Remember, each time you print a coupon before you need it, you then have to spend additional time to file the coupon. And when you eventually do need it, you have to figure out where you put it. Overall, printing too early makes for a lot of unnecessary back and forth. That's not to mention all the printer ink and extra paper used in the printing process.

Get in the habit of mostly printing coupons when you need them. Certain coupons you do need to print in advance, but most of them can be printed the same day you are heading out to shop. After you print, cut those along with the insert coupons you'll need for the shopping run. That will cut way down on the number of coupons you have to file.

How does this system work? Let's start with the coupons you need to print ahead of time. I suggest you print once monthly from the main sites, like Coupons.com, Red-Plum.com and SmartSource.com®. Remember, those are the sites offering coupons from several different manufacturers. After you have logged in to these sites, be sure to check off all the coupons that work for you, remembering to enter your zip code to see if any additional coupons are available in your area. Since these major sites typically reset at the beginning of each month, you need only print once and ignore them the rest of the time.

Print ahead only the coupons for items you use regularly—for example, if you see Charmin® coupons and that is the only brand your spouse likes, print it. After a while, you'll also be able to spot sale trends and know to print those, too. This takes time, however, so don't rush it and waste all your ink. Other than that, print coupons only as you need them. You can go back to these main sites if you know you missed one or two, but if you find it is becoming a habit, stop going back at all. Stick to the lazy couponing system: print most of your Internet coupons just before you head out for your shopping so you don't waste time filing them away and then trying to find them later.

Other coupons you have to print in advance because they are offered only until enough people download them and then the coupon disappears. From coupon links found on databases or from links on blogs and manufacturer sites, print as you discover the printable coupons. You can easily find the coupon you need buy searching any of the earlier suggested databases, such as DSM and KCL, or one you happen to favor, but keep in mind that Internet coupons from these kinds of sources tend to change quickly and often disappear altogether as manufacturers make them unavailable. Any individual links you discover searching through databases, or looking ahead on manufacturer specific sites, or even through couponing blog links, are usually time-sensitive and must be printed as you discover them.

For example, today as I write this, I found a $5 coupon link to K-Y® Brand Couples Lubricants products on the iheart Rite Aid® website. (You remember the iheart sites from page 178, chapter seven.) But by the time I found the link, clicking it directed me to a "Page not Found" screen, because the link had been removed. Other times like this, the link will send you to a "Promotion No Longer Available" page within the manufacturer's official website. Either way, the coupon will be gone. Therefore, if you find individual links for products you are likely to buy, print them right away.

Coupons on emails sent to you by companies work the much the same way, so print those, too. You'll be upset if you find that a coupon link is gone after saving it in your inbox for just the right moment. The exception is when the email is for an online coupon code rather than a coupon link, as the coupon code is a given phrasing for you to enter at online checkout and will have an explicit expiration. The emailed link, on the other hand, should be printed right away.

Couponing with phones can be tricky at first, because the technology for using your phone to access email is different from the one for downloading the coupon. But once you learn how, you'll realize nothing can be easier.

To coupon with your cellular phone, you simply need to use a mobile app to access them. Go to sites like Cellfire.com or AOL®'s shortcuts.com to get coupons sent to your cell. Thereafter, you can show cashiers your phone with the coupon image that the cashiers can scan.

If you try to access regular Internet printables through your mobile phone without the proper app, you will usually be redirected or have the opportunity to get those coupons by mail, like what's pictured below. As the actual image and a link to the image are two different things, emailed coupons should be printed to paper.

Another way to coupon via mobile technology is to use texting. Major stores like Target® have entered the technology game and now offer mobile coupons that you can get by joining their text messaging lists. The store will give you a code to text to them to start the process. After sign-up, the store will text you coupon codes in a coupon code image. To get your discount, show that image to the cashier so they can key it in their system.

The last kinds of coupons you should print in advance are those you find when you are ahead of the advertised sales by a week or so. (This will become easier the more familiar you get with your buying habits and their related sales cycles.) Now remember: make a list of exactly what you need ahead of time or don't bother to print. Treat these coupons the same way you would the manufacturers' coupons you print once a month.

For the most part, you should be printing just before you go shopping. Moments after I write my shopping list, I check the coupon databases for any match-ups, and print before leaving for the store. If a coupon from one of the inserts matches up, I also cut them out just before I leave, saving me the time of organization.

Keep in mind a simple principle: there is only so much you can do before extra effort becomes wasted effort. If you control how much time you put into couponing, you'll keep doing it. If you run too hard for a week or two, printing every coupon from every site you find, spending hours surfing the Internet or reading flyers, you run the risk of burning out and giving up couponing all together. In this case, slow and steady wins the race.

Finding Deals on the Go

Good time management also applies when you're shopping. When you're first starting out, I suggest you allow yourself an extra thirty minutes to shop at each store where you planned your run. Certain items that you collected coupons for will be unavailable once you get to the store, so give yourself ample time to either find a substitute item or rework the coupons you have on hand into a good deal. Other couponers want to buy the same items, and whoever gets to the store first seems to clear out the shelves. Remember those stockpiling people? Well, where do you think they buy their products? They run to the same stores you do, so be prepared to make switches in the moment. This will take practice. Though it will eventually become second nature, as a beginning couponer, you are better off allotting extra time and being prepared for the unpredictable.

STICK TO THE LIST

Avoid purchasing products you neither need nor intended to purchase. Over-buying is mostly made up of impulse purchases. Another reason people overbuy is they are preparing too far in advance for holidays or birthdays. If you get most of the items too early, you are more inclined to pick up some extra items just because.

When I first started using more than ten coupons on a single shopping run, I would become very frustrated if the items I had planned to buy were cleaned out. Even worse, if I had a transaction coupon around which my deal was built, I wasn't skilled enough to make quick substitutions. Now, making substitutions inside the store is easy for me. I know most product prices by memory and have a secondary list of sale prices and coupon match-ups rattling around in my brain, but that wasn't always the case. Please learn from my experience here and give yourself enough time to shop. That way you will be better prepared should you encounter a situation like this. By accounting for possible variables in your pre-time management, you avoid panic-stricken shopping.

Have you ever been at a store and found yourself panic-stricken? I have. How about getting home and realizing the five-minute run turned into an hour and a half? Yep, done that, too. In the beginning, my grocery store shopping trips took hours. I call those moments of lost time "shopping time-sucks." I really have walked aisles aimlessly searching shelves. I was not sure what happened to the time, or why I was in a tailspin. I was only sure of how much time I lost. My best guess is that I was too overwhelmed when I entered the store. Though I'd been shopping the same stores for years, I never really knew their layout. Did you know rice cakes are with cereal instead of popcorn? Or that microwave popcorn is often kept separate from the pre-popped bags you find in the chip aisle? I didn't then, but I do now. Since I've learned about product placement and where everything is, I no longer experience shopping time-sucks because of hunting all over the place. Most grocery stores have lists that number their aisles and tell where the most common items can be found. I suggest you stop by your grocer's customer service desk to see if they have one. If not, next time you go to the store, write down the general floor plan to make your next shopping trip easier.

Other times, you may see a coupon placed on the shelf next to an item. Do you want the item? Does the unexpected coupon mean you should substitute it for something else on your list? Do you add the item simply because it has a coupon attached? The answer to these questions is no. Don't change your plan because you see another deal. Just take the coupon to use later, when the item fills a legitimate need or want. Remember, there are endless possibilities for buying at a discount. Those new to using coupons may hem and haw over which is the best choice, sticking to a list or changing the game mid-play, but consistency and confidence have to be the factors on which you rely most. Avoiding changes to your plan, at this stage, will help you save time while shopping.

PULL BACK, LITTLE LADY

Christine is a couponing friend who went overboard. She was consumed with deal-chasing, having every imaginable coupon on hand, and stockpiling two freezers. As a result, she was wearing herself out. Her husband, though initially supportive, grew tired of her coupon frenzy. Christine spent hours prepping for sales and deals and still more hours at the stores. Did she forget a coupon? Panic. Did someone else buy up all of the items she sought? Panic. Was there an unadvertised sale? Panic. What finally happened when she prepared for possible variations? Calm. Oh—and she was in and out in a quarter of the time.

A second way to avoid shopping time-sucks is to shop off hours, especially when using more than $50 in coupons. When you walk around a store, especially a supermarket, with your coupon binder, people become curious. While most people will give only an inquisitive glance in your direction, some feel compelled to come up and ask about your savings techniques. I have been approached by many of these people, and I suspect you will, too. The encounters are usually brief and sincere, but they take time away from your shopping. It is easy to get lost in conversation and forget the task of couponing. Also, a conversation in the middle of shopping can ruin your flow and set you off track. Those minutes to talk, then to regroup, can easily turn into an hour lost before you know it. By shopping at odd times, you are less likely to be approached by an old friend or curious stranger, and thus you can control your in-store time more effectively.

CONCENTRATING AT THE STORE?

Cashiers aren't the only ones who make mistakes during busy shopping times. You can, too. I've been distracted by two noisy kids hanging off of my cart, and have mistakenly grabbed the wrong size, not the size specified on my coupon. I didn't realize my mistake until I was at the register cashing out, and by then it was too late to correct my mistake. I suffered by overpaying. Each time you pick out an item, make sure it's the right one.

Another reason for shopping off hours is to avoid causing delays when you check out. Cashiers and customers will both appreciate the courtesy. In addition, shopping during busy times may cost you money, because those are the times when cashiers make mistakes. It is easy to miss a coupon when the lines are bending around the corner. Also, busy shopping times are noisy shopping times. A beep from the scanner at the next register can sound like the beep from your register, causing the cashier to improperly scan your coupon.

When planning a trip to the grocery store, you always want to shop Friday through Sunday to maximize deals. Many stores run one- to three-day sales, when prices are discounted and after which return to normal. To make sure I catch all one-day shopping discounts, I prefer to grocery shop on Friday, but giving yourself the flexibility of the full three days is a little more forgiving. Believe me: it makes a big difference. By consistently shopping within that three-day period, you won't find yourself at a register wondering why chicken is ringing up $3.19/lb. rather than the $2.50/lb. advertised sale price.

For drugstores, the timing is different. You can shop at Rite Aid® and Walgreens® at the end of the week because their deals run weekly, and sometimes monthly. However, CVS often has one- to three-day sales, so you do best to shop there on Sunday. If you live near a non-24 hour store, you can actually shop Sunday's deals on Saturday night after 6:30 because that is when CVS stores change over the computers to the next morning's sales. The advantage to shopping on Saturday evening is that both weeks' specials and ExtraCare Bucks overlap for about an hour, so you can maximize any transaction coupons you have. Otherwise, it may be easier to stick to Sundays, when the newspapers with inserts are available. Either way, simply managing the timing of your shopping runs will see your savings increase.

Okay, so let's put the plan in action. You want in on the CVS deal for Toy Story 3 with purchase of Proctor & Gamble (P&G) products. You need to buy that DVD because your children love their Toy Story 1 and Toy Story 2 DVDs and because you are an awesome parent who has to round out the collection. As the deal states, if you buy $25 of Proctor & Gamble products, you will get the regularly priced ($19.99) Toy Story 3 DVD for just $3.99, which is a $16 savings. You put together two of the $1 coupons (Qs) for Charmin® and one $1Q (coupon) for Bounty that you clipped from your Proctor & Gamble A Year of Savings coupon book: the booklet Proctor and Gamble sent you

months ago for sending in some of your P&G receipts.

That brings your total to $27.90 for the toilet paper, paper towels, and Toy Story 3 DVD. Not bad, but you can do better.

Hoping to further defray some of the cost, you head to

CVS intending to also get the Bayer DIDGET™ Blood Glucose Monitoring kit at $29.99. CVS is offering ten ECBs (ExtraCare Bucks) with the purchase and you wisely printed the $25 off coupon from bayerdidget.com, making the purchase a $5.01 money maker (MM) you can apply to the *Toy Story 3*/Proctor & Gamble deal. But, when you finally get to CVS, there are no monitors left. What do you do then? Do you pay the full $27.90 for the purchase, look for unadvertised deals like the one on Cold Buster® Honey Lemon Warming Syrup that when used with a $2 coupon is still a small money maker, or do you simply quit and leave empty handed? I suppose your answer depends on how well you managed your prep and planned for in-store glitches.

Coupon Buddies

Having a coupon buddy doubles the sets of eyes checking the coupon websites and flyers. Do you have a friend who searches through sale racks each time you shop together? How about a spouse with a competitive nature? What about a sister-in-law, friend, or co-worker who already knows what you like?

A coupon buddy can also be someone with whom you share great deals or larger quantity purchases, thus lowering your costs and time spent shopping. I have a coupon buddy, Jenn, who looks through the ads at various stores where I don't regularly shop, and I do the reverse for her. Sometimes we cover the same store ads, too, gathering more information about sales and deals. Also, Jenn and I like different couponing websites and we have totally different styles: she prefers websites that have running dialogues, like Baby Center, while I prefer limited dialogue and clear lists like those offered at Deal Seeking Mom. All those differences and overlaps translate to greater savings because we've cast a broader net by covering more stores and advertised sales.

FAMILY TIME

Get your kids into the act, too! Preschoolers love to cut along dotted lines, so let their tiny hands do the coupon clipping and free your fingers. If you're teaching older children about the value of money, use them as coupon spotters while in the store. Have your teens help look for deals or coupon codes on the Internet.

Any family elders want to get in the action? Remember, cutting coupons is great for physical dexterity, and matching up the coupon to the item on sale is great for mental acuity, too.

For example, last night Jenn dropped me an email about a one-night sale at an online store where I've never shopped, Sally Beauty Supply®. Jenn caught a deal where, using three online coupons, I was able to get roughly $20 of free items delivered to my door along with free shipping. My actual cost was $1 and change, as I had to cover my Massachusetts state tax. The items I chose will make wonderful stocking stuffers for my nephew's girlfriend, and I would have completely missed the deal left on my own.

Earlier this year, Jenn was responsible for turning my eye to a Medco® Health online deal that spread through the couponing world in a matter of minutes. Medco Health was running a special sale that, when combined with very specific coupon codes, made $25 worth of items free. Couponers all over were claiming personal products, medicines, supplements and all sorts of things for free. I ordered my youngest son, Bradley, his very own kid-sized potty. Bradley just loved it. Thanks to Jenn, I paid nothing for the potty and I was also able to get some bath salts for myself.

Conversely, because I am terribly lazy and Jenn is not, I  give her all my reward codes for items like Coke, Huggies®, Pampers®, and Honest® Juice Drinks, which Jenn then enters online at their respective websites. Using the reward points, Jenn earns more coupons and sometimes prizes for herself. By working together, we cut our time spent searching for coupons in half—and access more steals and deals.

As a lone couponer, you can achieve savings well into the 50% range, but a coupon partner can raise that number upwards to 90%. All of my best non-grocery store deals have been through my couponing partnership with Jenn. Most of my success in preparing coupon match-ups to corresponding Christmas sales, Black Friday runs, and end of season sales all come from our teamwork. The greatest advantages come from teaming with a coupon buddy, and I think everyone serious about savings needs to find someone with whom she can partner.

Giving Up Your Time

Be sure to check those coupons and Internet printables you've already collected for their expiration dates every three to four months. Pull aside all of the expired coupons, but please don't throw them out. Instead, consider combining the expired coupons and any others you won't use and send them to our overseas military personnel. Remember, they can use the expired coupons in their commissaries.

Many of our enlisted soldiers and their families live paycheck to paycheck in general, often qualifying for food stamps, or finding it challenging to stretch dollars to meet their needs. Living overseas can make these hardships worse. In July 2009, Bryan Mitchell of Military.com wrote, "Military members and their families are using more food stamps than in previous years—redeeming them last year at nearly twice the civilian rate, according to Defense Commissary Agency figures. The agency reports that more than $31 million worth of food stamps were used at commissaries nationwide in 2008." Since assistance like food stamps is only available in the States and can't be used in overseas commissaries, it is particularly important for us to contribute our coupons.

In order to send coupons to accepting bases, first sort the coupons into food and non-food groups, trimming excess edges. Once overseas, someone on base will make sure the coupons are distributed at the commissaries where folks can use them. While the military prefers coupons within thirty days of expiration, most overseas commissaries accept coupons up to three months old, some even permitting coupons up to six months expired. A complete list of overseas commisary addresses is available at www.lazy couponer.com

ARE YOU READY TO MANAGE TIME EFFECTIVELY?

1. **What is time management's one simple rule?**
   a. Chase as many sales as possible.
   b. Shop the same store several times a week.
   c. There's always another sale.

2. **Good time management includes planning your time well and ...**
   a. Preparing for variables
   b. Shopping daily
   c. Overwhelming yourself

3. **How many stores did Margaret shop during Black Friday?**
   a. Four
   b. Fourteen
   c. Twenty-four

4. **How much time do I spend on couponing prep before I leave to shop?**
   a. Fifteen to twenty minutes
   b. Twenty to thirty minutes
   c. Five to ten minutes

5. How often do I recommend printing Internet printables from the three main sites?
   a. Monthly
   b. Weekly
   c. Daily

6. How often do I recommend printing Internet printables from coupon links or manufacturer websites?
   a. Monthly
   b. When you discover the printable
   c. Daily

7. Which pairing is not one of those suggested to avoid shopping time-sucks?
   a. Know your product placement and stick to your list.
   b. Shop off hours and talk to friends.
   c. Stick to your list and shop off hours.

8. Finish this sentence. Get a ...
   a. New desk to organize.
   b. Manager to help you shop.
   c. Coupon buddy.

9. What should you do with your expired coupons?
   a. Throw them out.
   b. Start a fire.
   c. Send them to our overseas military for use in their commissaries.

10. If you fail this quiz, you should?
   a. Relax. Breathe. Be confident you'll get it.
   b. Read the chapter again, then quit.
   c. Give up couponing and spend way too much money.

   Answers: 1. c, 2. a, 3. b, 4. a, 5. a, 6. b, 7. b, 8. c, 9. c, 10. a

CHAPTER 10

Keeping It Organized

B Y NOW YOU HAVE LEARNED JUST ABOUT everything about the world of couponing. You know the difference between the types of coupons. You know how to rack up big savings at the grocery stores. You know how to slay the drugstores. You even have found out how to find deeper discounts at the everyday discount stores.

Yet one key ingredient is missing: how you keep track of all the little bits of paper that add up to cash. In the end, your success will be determined by how well you organize. I'm too lazy to keep track of a complicated system that you might find confusing—and in the end self-defeating. So we'll look at some simple systems that will maximize both your time and your savings. You need to know how to organize your coupons both at home and when you go to the store. In addition, you can use a simple system to keep track of all the Internet databases you check before you head out.

While we're on the subject of organizing, I'd also like to discuss the back end of the process. Do you really have to buy in great quantities in order to realize true savings? I say no, absolutely not. I don't do it, and I would never advise you to do it. If you organize your little pile before you shop, you won't have to organize a gigantic pile after you shop.

Coupon Storage

To save big, you need a lot of coupons. That doesn't mean, though, that you need a lot of space to store them. Nor is there one right way to organize your coupons; just a system that works for you. I suggest trying a couple of different ways and deciding what best suits you. You might have seen the person at the checkout register who uses an overstuffed envelope or, if slightly more organized, those old-fashioned coupon holders with roughly a dozen pockets to keep coupons sectionalized. I believe there are better ways to file away those coupons, both for at-home organization and in-store use.

Many starting out couponing choose to use either the  pocket-sized accordion file or white envelopes for storage. The pocket style organizer usually has twelve pockets and you can divide the sections into stores or categories; it comes with pre-printed labels for the section dividers. You can also use the envelopes the same way, by writing the category name on front and using several envelopes together at a time. If this is the system you choose, you will likely outgrow it quickly and will need something more flexible. I suggest skipping the mini-accordion all together, because it takes too long to scan through each section of Qs when you need them. Depending on how much time you want to invest in couponing, you might just want to start your organization with more flexibility to grow into. It doesn't

seem very time efficient if you have to reorganize mid-way through your couponing journey.

My first secret is: I separate my system into two parts, one for home and one for shopping. I use a large accordion file case for inserts and a zipper binder for clipped coupons or **Internet Printables** (IPs). My accordion case is really too heavy to carry around, and since I don't need it for quick coupons while shopping, I keep it at home. Taking it with me would make the process more difficult, and by now you know I am not about that!

How do you use an accordion file? It is divided into many sections that allow me to keep the different types of inserts separate—SmartSource, Red Plum, P&G, General Mills—and if there are too many inserts, like extra Smart-Sources, to fit in just one section, then I use two next to each other. Within each section, the inserts are organized by date with the most recent in front of the others. I simply write the inserts date on the cover, making sure not to write on back of a coupon I may want to cut out. When I pull the inserts out, I pull a section at a time to ensure they always stay in order. However, I know what section to pull because the printer also includes the insert's date on its binding. I organize my *All You* magazines the exact same way as the inserts.

I also include any coupon booklets, like P&G's *A Year of Savings* booklet and any drugstore booklets—filed neatly in the case. I don't file anything that is weekly, like sales fly-

ers because once I glance at them, I am ready to recycle them. If you follow this system, you may want to use one of the sections for current flyers until looking them over is speedy and becomes second nature.

While my accordion case stays under my desk at home, the zipper binder travels with me. Actually, it hardly ever enters the house except when I am organizing the Qs. I leave it under the passenger seat in my car most days so I have access to it should I make an unexpected stop. Since

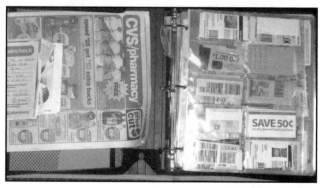

my zipper binder has a wonderful small outer pocket, that's where I keep extra loyalty cards. For example, I don't like the keychain loyalty card tags hanging down when I drive, so I put them in my binder in case I am shopping and forget the real card. Also, that section is great for storing a pack of gum and few dollars in cash, just in case I need either.

In the very front inside of the main part of the binder, I store a pen and the current flyer for the store where I am shopping with my list paper-clipped on, along with any coupons I have just cut out for the shopping run.

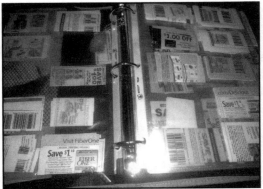

Next, the binder is sectionalized by tab dividers and organized in order of the supermarket aisles at my favorite store. That way if I come across an unadvertised sale or something I have missed, I can easily find any matching coupons I stored earlier. Within the sections I use both clear business card and sports trading card binder sleeves. Like coupons are lined up by date, those expiring first up front, and folded into the sectionalized sleeves. The only coupons that get organized within the compartments are those I have printed ahead of time off the Internet, loose coupons found in-store like Blinkies or tearpads, and any coupons I've received from my coupon buddy or the manufacturers themselves. All loose manufacturer coupons, no matter where I may use them, get stored in the zipper binder. CRTs and Catalina Qs, however, get wrapped around my loyalty cards and slid into the credit card compartments in my wallet. The rest of my coupons remain unclipped and filed away in the accordion folder until moments before I leave for the store.

After the binder sections organized by grocery aisles, I use the same filing system to keep all non-food coupons, such as personal care and toy Qs. The less likely I am to use the coupon, the more likely it is to be near the end. Following the non-food coupons, I have created an additional section for Restaurant.com® gift certificates, guest passes to the gym, wholesale shopping places, and children's entertainment passes. Items like that are placed in clear plastic page protectors at the end of the binder.

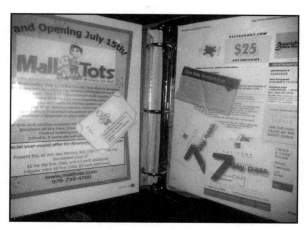

While any binder will do, I suggest you get one with a zipper because coupons are as sneaky as Leprechauns and escape whenever they can. Without a zippered binder you may find yourself in the middle of the store with coupons trailing behind as they drop to the floor. Oh, those naughty Qs!

Remember my coupon buddy Jenn? She stores everything in a coupon bag, stacking unclipped and labeled inserts together. Within the bag, she uses envelopes and Ziploc® bags for loose Qs. So you can try it my way, or Jenn's way, and if either way works for you, go with it. There are probably as many techniques as there are people. I suggest searching YouTube for "Coupon Organization" for other ideas. Or, you can go to YouTube to see me demonstrate my methods of coupon organization! (Go to www.thelazycouponer.com to see links.) How you organize really doesn't matter as long as you do organize.

One single point in keeping track of coupons is more important than all the others. Even though Jenn and I organize differently, we both follow one golden rule: don't clip until you need the Q!

In particular, stop clipping the inserts. Really! Every time you check a coupon database or blog, the information to finding the coupon is given by the insert's name and date, such as SmartSource 09/10. If you cut up all your inserts, how will you be able to find it? You won't. I don't care what order you put your inserts in, whether they are all in a box, binder or bag, but keep inserts whole! Never cut coupons until you need them. This is the one part of your personalized system you must follow. The rest is yours.

Information Storage

I suggest utilizing a toolbar folder bookmarked for the sites you regularly visit on the Internet. To build your online coupon folder, you need to add and organize your bookmarks. First type the URL—website address—into the address bar, and once the website loads, click the Book-

marks tab above. Depending on your browser, you need to select "add bookmark" or "bookmark this page," choose where it is to go, and click done. Do this for every coupon site you regularly visit. Then, to organize, go back into the Bookmarks tab and click on "organize bookmarks" or "show all bookmarks" where you can add a folder—mine is named "Coupon Sites"—and drag the bookmarked addresses into it. Then you'll have created a totally organized drop-down folder of the sites you regularly use, making the online coupon hunt even easier.

Keep current CAT info in a simple Word or Pages document. If you grocery shop weekly at a CAT store, you may want to keep the file right on your desktop. Set up the document in order of CAT date, adding newer CATs to the top as you come across them. For example, suppose you get new CAT info from a Catalina dispenser at checkout. When you get home, type the details into the computer file and throw away the little paper. That way, you won't need to keep track of the paper and you will be less likely to lose the information. Do the same with CAT ads you find in your circulars. For those you discover searching the couponing blogs, simply cut and paste the information from their lists into your document. Do not rely on bloggers to keep complete lists for you, because you need to remember that CATs are shopper-driven and your shopping habits might trigger a CAT that doesn't work for someone else. Keeping a list that includes information from others as well as what you physically get in the store is better. That way, you have a complete list compiled from many sources.

For reference, look at this example of a CAT document. Notice the information is organized by the date each CAT starts. If this were my CAT list, I'd enter in any new information as I'd get it, making sure to delete the expired ones before closing out of the document.

KEEPING YOUR CAT LIST

Post® Select Cereal 3/26–4/12
B2G $1.00
B3G $2.00
B4G $3.00

Kellogg's® Cereal and Milk Cat 3/25–4/16
Buy any three or more Kellogg's cereals 12 oz or larger,
   any flavor
buy 3–4, get one free gallon
buy 5–6, get two free gallons
buy 7 or more, get three free gallons
All free milk coupons are good on any brand, any flavor
   up to $4.19 per gallon

Dog Snacks, 3/22–4/18
(Milk-Bone®, Jerky Treats®, Pup-Peroni®, Snausages®,
   Meaty-Bone®)
Buy 2, get $1.00 OYNO
Buy 3–4, get $2.00 OYNO
Buy 5 or more, get $3.00 OYNO

McCormick® food color or extract CAT from 3/19–4/11.
B2G $1.50
B3G $2.50

CAT coupons that will last only for a short time, like week-only CATs, shouldn't be added to your CAT list if they fall within the current time period. Do include the information if the CAT is still to come, since that is a good reference source for later.

Also, don't bother to contact Catalina Marketing about CAT information, as they have no prior knowledge of upcoming CATs. They have an enormous database and too many retail clients to be able to give upcoming or current shopping offers to you. They simply cannot access the information requested, so don't push. Keep your own list and don't waste time calling people who can't help you.

Product Storage

To stockpile, or not to stockpile? That is the question. While most coupon crazies preach stockpiling, I say let it go. This is the main difference between the ways most other people and I coupon. I realize the same success in savings without all the effort. Stockpiling is like a gateway drug to hoarding. And, unless you hope to someday tiptoe around boxes ready to fall on your head, it is totally unnecessary. Merriam-Webster's primary definition for a stockpile is "a reserve supply of something essential accumulated in a country for use during a shortage." Your family, my friend, is not its own country, nor is all that stuff you are storing really essential. Having a few toothpastes or body washes on hand is great, as they take up little cabinet space, but really, anything more than that just complicates life.

I'm not talking about a single backup of all the items your family regularly uses. I concede the logic in that, especially since you need to buy two items in any BOGO sales. But storing 50 rolls of paper towels and 22 cereal boxes in your garage doesn't make any sense. Beyond the inconvenience of crowding your living space, stockpiling creates a need to inventory items and to track expiration dates. I have worked in a retail store, and I can tell you from hard-earned experience that inventory is a huge hassle. Who wants to add stress to our lives? Not me. Remember, I told you couponing was to simplify your life, not complicate it. So, get the food out of the garage and drive your car back in.

The problem grows even worse when extra food is stockpiled inside the house. Here is a picture of my friend's pantry. She really is a wonderful friend because she is letting me share this with you. What you can't see is that this is an old stairwell next to the kitchen that was blocked off because of their addition and now serves as a pantry. Why do I tell you that? Because, in order to reach the bottle of Hunt's ketchup on that high-up shelf, I would have to stand on my tiptoes and lean way in. I have not the faintest idea how I'd get to the cans above or deep behind the ketchup. While my dear friend, who hopefully remains my friend after reading this, insists she knows exactly what she has in her pantry, I think she is mistaken. There is just too much stuff. Even if she were to rotate it all for inventory, I fear she'd never use it all by its expiration date. Her argument for stockpiling so much is that she never runs out of anything she needs—except for the morning we were supposed to make banana bread and she was mysteriously out of flour.

I do run out of products, which is supposedly the carnal sin for someone trying to save money. However, the shortages don't seem to affect my savings and I keep my pantry uncluttered. Here is a picture that I took within ten minutes of returning home from taking the picture of my friend's pantry. My pantry is two feet deep and most items sit in a

single row with nothing behind them, as you can see. I thought about removing my reusable bags and recycling from the bottom before taking the picture, but then I realized I had to be fair. I mean, she didn't get the chance to clean up before I snapped the picture of her pantry, so why should I?

I should admit that the very night I took this picture I decided to make barbecue chicken for my husband, Justin, when I discovered I was totally out of barbecue sauce and had to whip it up from scratch. Fortunately, it only took me two minutes to make and Justin actually preferred it. Too bad he didn't have any banana bread to go along with it.

While there are exceptions—certainly a large family has different considerations—unless your family budget or extended size dictates a need to stock and store, don't do it. For an average family, I suggest you try to gift or donate your couponing excess. Consider it your opportunity to give back. The process of sharing is very rewarding, and it frees you from treating your home like a small store: limit your keep extras to a few small items.

Free pet food can be dropped in the bins where you walk out at most grocery stores, and churches and shelters alike usually take non-perishable, non-frozen foods and personal care items. Bring a bag of Depend® Undergarments to a church or soap and razors to a shelter, and you'll be treated like a rock star. By following the *Lazy Couponer* method of shopping and saving, you'll likely wind up with some excess in one area or another—whether it's from buying filler items or special manufacturer promotions—and you'll still be saving lots of money at the register. Start shopping for personal gain and end up giving back in the process! I can't imagine a more encouraging reason to start couponing.

As lazy as I am, I make a charitable drop-off once a month at my convenience, so it is a practice you can do, too. Also, your in-laws, neighbors, and kids' teachers might benefit from little packages of goodies, as well. Everybody wins!

HOW DO YOU ORGANIZE?

1. What must you first organize?
   a. CAT information
   b. Coupons
   c. Product

2. My accordion folder is used to store ...
   a. Loose coupons
   b. Internet printables and inserts
   c. Inserts, *All You*, and coupon booklets

3. Where do I store loose coupons and Internet printables?
   a. In a zipper binder
   b. In an accordion folder
   c. In a plain white envelope

4. To be successful you must use ...
   a. Anyone's coupon storage technique—just organize!

b. Jenn's coupon storage technique

c. My coupon storage technique

5. What is the one coupon organization rule you must follow?

a. Sort by date

b. Sort by source

c. Don't clip until you need the Q

6. What is the suggested way to organize CAT info?

a. Relying on online couponing blog lists

b. A Word or Pages document

c. Keeping all your CAT printouts

7. Internet couponing sites should be stored ...

a. Together in a bookmark folder

b. On the hard drive

c. Why bother to store them again?

8. Should my friend whose pantry I photographed remain my friend?

a. Yes

b. Yes, as well as both answers a and c

c. Yes

9. To what is the suggested amount of backup items you should limit your item?

a. Ten

b. Two

c. Twenty-two

10. Consider what as an alternative to stockpiling?

a. Trashing any extra items

b. There's no alternative to stockpiling

c. Donation

Answers: 1. b, 2. c, 3. a, 4. a, 5. c, 6. b, 7. a, 8. b, 9. b, 10. c

Index